As Told To Me

As Told To Me

My Connection to the Spirit Realm Through
The Ultimate Chat Line

Peter W Watson

All rights reserved. No part of this publication may be reproduced or transmitted in any form or by any means, electronic or mechanical, including photocopy, recording, or any information storage and retrieval system without the written permission of the publisher.

Cover photo by Peter Watson

Whipper Press

88 Dean Ave Guelph On Canada N1G 1L6

pete@joyessence.on.ca

ISBN 978-0-9867958-0-0

10 9 8 7 6 5 4 3 2 1

To my

Spiritual Guide

"SARA"

CONTENTS

From the Editor   *i*

Acknowledgments   *ii*

Foreword   *iii*

Introduction   *v*

In the Beginning   1

The Ouija Board   3

Automatic Writing   4

My Guide Sara   8

Inspirational Writing   9

The Daily Messages   11

In Conclusion   145

About the Author   149

Have you ever listened to the voice within?

To some it is never heard.

To others it is overlooked.

For me, it has changed a great deal of my life.

It is said that the voice is there

for each of us to hear.

Why then, do so few listen?

Peter W Watson

From the Editor

It has been a privilege to assist Peter in the preparation of this manuscript. He has been gifted with unusual insights, as well as unusual access to other dimensions; and, he needed only some extra tools and a bit of encouragement to bring these messages into the material realm for those who are receptive.

For me it has been an opportunity and learning experience with respect to book publishing in the internet world. I have also benefited from the new-found friendship of Pete and his wife Joy.

Please note that the sometimes archaic language of certain spirits has been left unaltered, so as to preserve the authentic quality of the communications. At times, statements are made which appear rather arcane, and neither the author nor myself has the final word as to their sense and meaning. They are to be taken as is for the reader to discern.

Lorraine Speer

Acknowledgments

I am deeply indebted to the assistance of Lorraine Speer, who came quite unexpected into my life at a time when I was in need of some expertise on just what it would take to put this manuscript into shape for publishing. It was, as I would find out, to be a very large and demanding chore.

As a librarian and as an English specialist, Lorraine's contribution was greatly appreciated. Considering Lorraine had many things requiring her attention at the time, she still happily made the time to assist in this endeavor.

Thanks Lorraine.

I would also like to thank my granddaughter, Ashley, for her assistance in setting up the manuscript into the computer. You were there when I needed you Ashley.

Thank you.

A special thanks goes to my wife Joy who often set aside her own work to help me in finally finishing this endeavor that I started over thirty years ago. Now that it is finally going to print I won't be pestering you to get me out of my computer problems any longer.

Love you

Foreword

I am very proud to call Peter Watson my Grandfather. He is truly a remarkable man in his own right.

Growing up, I was always fascinated by the stories that I heard from my mother of the many experiences she had with Peter, her father, and I always wanted to know more, maybe even experience for myself the gifts I truly believe that he has. There are many journal entries missing from this book; the reason for this is because the Guides with whom he was speaking asked him to only publish the messages they felt would be of guidance to those (you) reading this book, and that his personal experiences and messages were only for him to read. I feel it is important; however, to tell you that from my experience, and those in my family that many of his personal messages did, in fact, come about as predicted, including his ability to be a healer. Through the years he has helped many who suffered from ailments, including my mother, many strangers and myself.

You might say that Peter is a very modest man and does not wish to tell those reading this book of all the wonderful things he accomplished with these gifts; however, I feel compelled to inform readers of his very special abilities, so they can feel connected to the messages he has recorded. These journals were compiled from November

1979 until November 1980; however, it has taken 30 years for these messages to be published. I feel that I was meant to assist Peter in organizing this book for publishing (as his Guides had requested so strongly). I was not born until 1983, so it would make sense that it has taken so long for this to happen. This feeling only intensified when I was reading the entry dated three years before my birth on November 5th, 1980. It said amongst other things that *"your books will take more time than you realize"* and that *"this book must be written."* I have taken on the gift of *automatic writing*, which is what this type of communication is called, when you allow the spirit world to connect through you and write, using your hand to send messages from the Other Side.

I am very passionate about this book and the messages that are inside. As this book will tell you, some of the readers will feel this collection is fictitious and will brush it off as such; however, some of you will share Peter's experience in your own way. I feel that many of you will be given the hope, strength and faith that you are seeking in your specific life circumstances after you finish reading. I am truly blessed to have Peter Watson as my Grandfather and it has been a pleasure helping him to put this book together. I hope you will all enjoy these readings as I have.

-Ashley Baldwin

Introduction

My story evolves from my unexpected introduction to the Spiritual world, which was very hard for me to accept when it started happening. At that time, changes began that would influence the rest of my life. The "Supernatural", or the Spiritual existence, was something that I had little knowledge of, and little interest in. However, it was now my time to begin listening to the "voice within".

What you are about to read may seem very unlikely, but when you start to delve into the "hereafter" you never know for sure where you may end up. In my case, it opened the door to an experience that at times left me wondering just where that boundary line is between life today, and death tomorrow. Also, it opened up a line of communication with a group of extremely interesting entities who just happen to reside on the "other side".

As someone with very little Christian upbringing, I was left wondering why this was happening to me. What did I have to offer this union? I knew nothing of the "after life" that was spoken of in books hidden from view in the local book stores; however, here I was sitting and communicating with someone that was telling me they were from the next dimension. We have all heard references to that tiny small voice within, but when such a voice becomes an everyday occurrence, believe me, it can and does change your life.

A new routine is hard to adapt to when you are middle aged and looking for a break from endless demands on your time. I now found myself spending two to three hours every day conversing with the voices from the other side. How, you might ask, did this come about? Was it just a stroke of fate that put me in the right place at this time? Or could it have been that I was selected for this strange connection to the *Hereafter*? The confusion of this all happening right out of the blue put me very much on the defensive. At times, it felt like an intrusion in my life.

Before this all started to happen, I felt that I was just a normal everyday guy, going about making a living and raising a family. Born in the city of Toronto, Canada during the 1930's, with three sisters and five brothers, things were not a bed of roses. At quite a young age I moved with my family to Utopia. Oh yes, there is such a place. At that time, my father was in the Canadian army, stationed at Camp Borden, just west of the Town of Barrie in the rural area of Utopia. In fact, my first school was SS#9 Essa, a three mile walk by road, or two miles across the farm fields. The farm house I lived in was a three story, cold and scary place. By the end of World War II, my family had moved twice more - once to the village of Shanty Bay (my Grandmother would send our birthday cards to Shanty Town) and then on to Orillia, just another 22 miles further north.

The bulk of my schooling was in Orillia, finishing up at West Ward Public School. I was just 14 years old when I started to work for a living. My first job was at the local Dodge-DeSoto dealers, then on to a stint with the Nash car dealer. By age 17 I was married with a family of my own and needed a better paying job, so I hired on at an automotive machine shop and learned a trade.

With the loss of an infant son, I turned away from what little connection I had with God and the church. I felt betrayed, and that feeling stayed with me for many years. With the passing of time, I found myself sitting in a development circle with a group of Spiritualists, and looking for enlightenment. It was through this group that I was given the opportunity to try my hand at "Automatic Writing". What followed over the next year was quite profound in the sense that I found myself getting into some very deep and unfamiliar waters.

As you read this book, I would ask that you be patient with respect to the early spirit contacts, as I was being educated by a group of departed Souls who wished to give mankind some answers to many of our questions. This did require a great deal of patience on both sides, as I was having enormous problems accepting that this could really be happening. Just how often are you faced with this kind of a situation in life?

I slowly did begin to accept the possibility, and began to look forward to what new enlightenment would be presented each day. As time passed, the messengers would change, and the depth of the messages increased greatly. You will find that many messages are attributed to specific, named spirits, while some others bear no names at all. Names, I was often told, made little difference to the content of these messages. I did, however, build a bond with a few of the entities that contributed on a daily basis; so much so, that they seemed to become members of my family.

Another thing I wish to draw to your attention is the dates attached to the messages. You will find that there are many dates not accounted for. At those times I received some very personal messages that were for myself, or another family member, and these would have had no interest to others. Although there are many repetitious entries, I was still able to take something away from every one.

I feel quite privileged to have been chosen to receive this information. Most of us can only speculate as to what will happen when we face the inevitable reality of leaving this earthly home and journeying to the next plane. I now look at the possibility with optimism. I no longer deny the possibilities, but rather, feel comfortable in knowing that there is something beyond death.

Many times there are references made to healings by my

guides. I would like to explain, as best I can, how these healings took place. I am not an expert on this subject, and had no training in this healing art. You may be sure it was quite an experience to find that I could actually get many satisfying results. I came to understand that this is a gift that humans have shared, since time immemorial, with the aid of Spirit Guides, to help their fellow humans. The healer works on the energy field around the body in various ways, including the laying on of hands. There is, however, one other absolutely essential ingredient, that of prayer. It is my belief that this is the most important one of all.

Personally I have had many gratifying experiences with what I will refer to as Spiritual Healing. I have also had the fortunate experience of working alongside my wife, in her role as a massage therapist. This gave me the opportunity to see the results of these healing sessions first hand

So, how did this affect me? When I say that the overall experience has changed my life, it is not easy to put into words. How do you describe not only conversing with the dearly departed but also following their suggestions to help others? You may well wonder how I look at Christianity now that I am on speaking terms with angels. This much I am sure of - God, in his mercy, must approve of what I have been doing as I have not been struck with thunder bolts after all these years.

I do believe that I look at matters with a different perspective. I feel more comfortable in knowing there is much more to LIFE than what I have experienced here on earth. Just the thought of life carrying on in a different dimension, and the prospect of life eternal, imbues my everyday life with greater significance.

I was told on more than one occasion, in fact many times, that I have spent a number of lifetimes here on earth. It seems that I have had a hard time learning, and have had to repeat this earthly visit, trying to find my way. Perhaps this time I will get it right.

The spiritual, or supernatural, can be an exciting part of one's life. However, it can also be quite frightening, if you are unprepared. I say this because not all messages that came to me were loving and tender. In fact, some were downright scary. When you think about God's love, and his band of angels, you would not expect, nor would you be prepared to receive, a message with cruel intent. During a year or more of receiving messages on a daily basis, at times I would also receive messages from a much lower form of entity. I would be told that I was to be killed that very day as I drove home from work. How do you handle a thing like this? By not buying into it, was the answer I found. I made up my mind right from the first cruel message that the sender was a low level spirit that was trying to cause trouble. I just felt that with all the loving spirit Guides I had around me, it was impossible for these misguided messages to hold any true meaning; therefore, I ignored them.

While I was compiling this book, the content of these daily messages moved from the immediate, personal realm to a broader look at life and death. Although my belief in a superior power was somewhat limited, I did have a feeling that there was more to life than what we normally experience. Having had more than one brush with death perhaps led me to experience this transmission with an open mind.

Spiritually, the church can be seen to reside in the body and soul of the participant, for God dwells in every man. I must say that I never truly grasped the full meaning behind some of my messages until I started rewriting them into this book. Others, I must also admit, are still beyond my comprehension. As I sat many a night until the wee hours of morning compiling these pages, a feeling of not being alone was quite prevalent. Somehow I have to accept the fact that I alone could not have made this book a reality. At times I would lose sight of reality and think, "My God I am writing a book". How wrong I was. I know now that, was it not for my guides and the encouragement of my family and close friends, this book would never have materialized.

Thinking back on what took place, I find that I was given much more than a few words on paper. I was given a greater understanding of life and of myself. When I was down in spirits, I was lifted by the daily messages. When I needed compassion, I found this also. A fine example of this was the way that the daily messages brought a definite understanding of life after death. The repetition of the subjects, every incarnation linked with the passing of life from the flesh to the spiritual plane, was leading me up to one of life's sadder moments. It was at the height of these messages, when the word arrived that my sister had lost her battle with cancer. As shocked as I was, I slowly began to realize that the messages had been preparing me for this turn of events. Man is never alone, unless he wants to be.

I know now that this has been an experience that I would never have wanted to miss, although I must admit I still find myself wondering, "Why me?" Surely there are many others far more deserving than I to have had this experience. When looking back into the many messages I received, if I knew then that I would write a book, I would never have believed it, but then again, do we really control our own destiny? Writing a book was mentioned several times and you would think I would have been listening. I still wonder after this all happened, could a similar inspiring force have been behind the renowned authors of many of the literary masterpieces of the past? One does have to wonder why some seem to hold such wisdom. Surely it comes easier the second and third time around. Reincarnation perhaps?

Man strives to unlock many doors, but usually only with scientific approaches. He does not let his vision take him to the next plane. Wouldn't life take on a different outlook if we removed the skepticism from our quest? Surely the complexities of life could be changed to allow man time to consider the other possibilities. In one message, the guides indicate that *"the stumbling blocks are put there by man himself"*. What does this mean? If you let your thoughts wander a little, would you not admit to wanting a more meaningful life? The pressures of modern living can often hold us back from experiencing a truly rewarding spiritual life. The deeper meaning is there to be discovered.

When you consider the overwhelming amount of illness that is evident on this earth, you have to wonder if there is another way to cure these ills than to take endless pills. Though healing is mentioned in my writings on many occasions, one thing should be stated very clearly: the total healing of body and soul will only come through God's love. Perhaps medical science should dwell a little longer on the human spirit and not just its bodily functions.

It is my hope that through the many messages that I have received, others will grasp a little more understanding of life. You may have heard it said, *"We are not here for a long time, but for a good time. Could it be that we are actually here many times?*

In The Beginning

My personal background had little Christian teaching. My venture into Sunday school was brief as a child, and then I only attended church on the odd occasion. I point this out only as it is of the utmost importance that it is clearly understood that my childhood and adulthood were not spent embracing a Christian belief. My own conscious belief, however, was that there was a superior power that had put this whole Universe into being, and was also the one holding it together.

As a child, I had played at making a table talk. This was also referred to as "Table Tipping". I should explain this to those who are unfamiliar with the phrase. A small table, preferably a three-legged one, is chosen for this act of telling fortunes. To do this, I would ask questions and have the table give the answers. Sounds rather odd, does it not? As I had spent many an hour at this pastime in past years, I can verify that answers have been received by using this method. The answers are obtained by asking for a tap of the table's leg upon the floor. The method I used was to ask for one tap for a "yes" answer and two taps for a "no". Although amusing and somewhat entertaining, I stopped this form of communication while still a youngster, but did pick it back up later in life, as a fun hobby with friends who were interested.

I have experienced many brushes with death that have made me wonder why I am still here. One in particular, I would like to share with you in this book. It was in the early

1950's and I was on the side of the road fixing my car with the hood propped open. The passengers were inside, as well as more friends in a car behind mine waiting for me to get back on the road. As I went about my work under the hood, I looked up when I heard a car in the distance, thinking to myself "help is coming". As the sound grew closer, I thought that the car wasn't going to stop to help after all, as it was moving at a high rate of speed. I looked up through my windshield to see the lights of the car approaching, and then looked back down into my hood. As I peered up once more the lights had disappeared and all of a sudden everything went black. When I gained my senses back, I was standing on the side of the ditch facing the highway. My car was about 150 feet down the road. You see, the car I had seen was being driven by a drunk driver, who smashed into the car behind mine, propelling my car down the road with great force, while I stood on the sidelines unaware that this had occurred. I knew for certain that I should have been run over with my own vehicle that night, since I had been standing right in front of my car; but, for some reason, I was not harmed in the least, and did not recall moving. The only other indication of something extraordinary having occurred was my missing wristwatch that one of the police officers found by chance in the snow bank. I knew that my life had been spared, but to this day, I wonder why.

As Told To Me

The Ouija Board

Many years later, I was confronted with the "Ouija board". Although it is not looked on very favourably, because of the possibility of attracting evil spirits, it played a great part in the preparation for my advancement to later abilities. The Ouija, as had the table, gave me hours of interesting communication with someone or something non-corporeal. I always approached the use of this instrument as merely a form of entertainment and did not take seriously the many tales that unfolded. An open mind on the subject is a must. Many people have gullibly accepted as truth all messages they have received from the Ouija board; however, it is advisable to be cautious in its use, as you do not really know what type of entity is coming through. God gave us a mind of our own, and in such situations, a person must discern carefully whether the communication that has been received is something that should be accepted.

Regardless of the question of its authenticity, on many occasions the Ouija revealed something that did indeed come true. Again, I must emphasize that an evil entity can come to you in this manner very easily. Had I known what would come to pass in the future, I would have conducted myself quite differently. Good or bad, I cannot help but think that without my venture into this type of contact with the supernatural, I would not have gone on to my present endeavors of conversing with the spirit plane. It was after another evening of trying the Ouija board, that I once again tried the table. This was done as a test to satisfy the urge to see whether I could still perform this odd feat. To my amazement, the power that I possessed that evening far exceeded any that I had had for many years. I had the feeling of connecting to a new, and much more powerful, internal force, which was now at my command.

Automatic Writing

The following evening, I sat with pencil in hand to attempt *"automatic writing"* for the first time. A friend of mine, who had already experienced this type of contact with the Spiritual plane, introduced it to me, and I found it to be a frightening experience at first. It is not easy to describe; however, I would like to try and explain in my own way what happened that first time.

With pencil in hand, I sat at the large table in my family room, and, while all was quiet, I asked out loud if there was *"someone"* who might have a message for me. To my amazement, my right hand (which was holding the pencil) began to draw tiny circles on the paper. It moved slowly at first, but then with speed and force, until I broke the lead. Gathering up a number of pencils, I once again started drawing these uncontrolled scribbles. It was very similar to the writing exercises we performed in grade school many years ago. Gradually the erratic force slowed inside my hand, and words began to form, spelling out a message that I shall remember to my dying day. *"Peter is unhappy he does not have a grave stone."* These words tore me to my very soul, as it held a message that was truly meant for me. Eighteen years prior to this experience, my youngest son Peter Jr., had died as an infant. To this day, a small marker is all that indicates his gravesite. Many times, I had wanted to place a headstone, but it has never been done. You may be able to appreciate how overwhelmed I was, as this first message held such personal meaning.

The message carried on with a few more words about my family, and then my contact on the Spiritual plane connected me with someone else who knew me very well. It was my deceased father-in-law. This was the first of many sessions that I would have with him. I would like to refer back to the Ouija board for a moment. He had also made contact with me during those events, but I wasn't entirely convinced of his authenticity, because of my reservations about the Ouija board. Until the writings started, serious thought was never put to the context of the messages, but now, as messages were coming through my very own hand with such force, it was hard to deny them. But was this for real? I questioned repeatedly, as I tried to control my emotions. I soon became convinced that I was communicating with the spirit that never dies.

Over the next few weeks, my departed father-in-law relayed his messages to me at a more controlled pace through my writing. By this I mean that I was no longer forced to write at breakneck speed whatever he wished to convey. At one point, when stopping yet again to re-sharpen a pencil that was broken, the impatient spirit stopped his message and relayed to me the following: *"Get a damn pen"*. This manner of speaking did not entirely surprise me, as the man I had known in life was never gentle. His gruff exterior was very evident in the manner by which he spoke and acted while alive, and also now in spirit. Some of his messages left me a bit shaken, as time and again, they held an urgent significance for another family member.

Finally, he relayed the message that he would cease to communicate with me. Questioning this, I was told that I was far too emotional for him to continue. You see, he had a way of bringing a message to me, which could easily be construed as having a harsher meaning than he actually intended, due to his gruff personality. My father-in-law was not meant to be my Spiritual Guide; however, it was through his messages that my attention had been gained. Once he ceased communication, I was left with a feeling of unsettled emotion.

I mentioned earlier that I questioned myself many times on the authenticity of the writings and the information they contained. To the uninformed, the Spiritual world is very hard to comprehend and accept. I felt as though my own subconscious mind might be bringing this forward. To my delight, I was destined to meet a man who was an author of a few books of his own on this subject. When I explained to him my feelings of doubt as to the writings being sent to me from the Spiritual plane, he assured me that it was his own experience to have accepted many writings in the same fashion. I transitioned from automatic writing to a very different type of writing. As I mentioned before, I lacked the type of background to converse easily on the subject so it was a great relief to find someone else who had experienced the same phenomenon, and who was far better acquainted with the subject. With this person's encouragement to continue the daily sessions, I now looked forward, with greater interest, to receiving the messages.

The author I speak of was a professor at the college my son was attending at that time. My son happened to mention to the professor that his father was involved with a group of spiritualists and was involved with Automatic Writing.

The professor, a parapsychologist, along with his wife, also a parapsychologist, had written some books on the subject. He indicated a desire to meet with me to discuss my progress with the writing. This meeting would involve a two hundred mile drive for him in mid-winter. The meeting lasted five hours and I came away feeling much better about my involvement. When I explained to him that I was worried that perhaps my own subconscious mind was playing tricks on me, he disagreed, and told me I had a gift that very few people possess, and I should definitely pursue it.

The professor was not the last person to encourage me to continue with the writing; however, his emphasis on parting, that this was a rare opportunity, and one that very few would ever have, made a profound impact on me. I credit this meeting with putting me soundly back on track with the writing.

    As I think back on it all now, had the first spirit contact not been with my father-in-law, someone who knew me well, I probably would not have continued. Regardless of the frightening aspect of spirit communication, I was bolstered by the familiar contact, and resolved to carry on with the next phase.

Now it was time for a more advanced spirit to initiate communication and become my Spiritual Guide over the next eight months.

My Guide, Sara

The first message that I received through this new Guide was signed "Sara". Little did I realize the depth of the messages that would follow. Over the ensuing months, Sara and I formed a bond like you would have with a member of your own family, or a dear and close friend. Her words left me feeling very secure in the knowledge that the Spiritual realm has a great deal to do with our lives. The writing that followed gave an insight into life and death that I had never considered before. The sincerity with which the messages flowed lifted me to the greatest heights I have ever felt. At the same time, being part of this truly unbelievable process made me feel very small and humble. The names used to sign off at the bottom of the daily sessions were some that I recognized, while others were unknown to me. Sara, however, was to be my main Spiritual contact.

Her encouragement to follow a daily routine with the writing, and to retain the text of each, gave me a strength I had never known. A concept my Guide dwelled upon very seriously was reincarnation. Life and its many cycles through reincarnation came to hold a strong fascination for me. To sit and write automatically about such a thing, when I previously knew nothing about it, seemed to be like stepping into a different world.

Inspirational Writing

I sat each day at 7am, and found myself knowing each word as it was written on the page. It was like writing a story, knowing each word as it came to me, before I wrote it down. However, the text of each day's lessons held such a deep spiritual meaning that I could not have made this up in my own mind.

Soon I was to meet another group of people in a development class, whose encouragement meant a great deal to me, and helped with my progress in what was now developing as *"Inspirational Writing"*. Inspirational Writing was explained to me as receiving in thought form, a message sent by a spirit on the next plane. In the weeks and months to follow, I received messages from many Spiritual Guides. God was spoken of in almost all of my daily sessions now. The writing was to be done at a set time of day where I could be alone with my thoughts.

In truth, I had not come this far without a great deal of inward doubt. The writing continued; however, a new pattern was being set. I told myself the subconscious was playing tricks on me, but once again the contents of the daily writings left little doubt that I did not possess the spiritual background to write the words I was putting on paper. To write a simple letter had always been something I would shy away from, but now, here I was writing the text for a sermon that could easily be preached from many a pulpit. How strange it was to be given this kind of communication when, in fact, I had never read the Bible. The depth of feeling I attained from the writings gave me an inner peace that I had never before experienced. While life now began to take on new meaning, the thought of death no longer seemed so final. Now I was to learn of life after death.

As Told To Me

The Daily Messages

Now I had the contents of the many days' writings, and it was from these writings I was told that this book was to be written. In fact, I was told on so many occasions that I was to set aside time to write this book, that I finally felt compelled to actually do so. I believe that I held off because of the fear of not knowing how to go about it. What follows is the text of many months of transmissions as they were written through me. It may well seem impossible to you, but this is the way it was *"told to me"*.

GEORGE: You are not trying to write as often as you should, as sometimes you are very hard to get. Your mind is always full of some thoughts, and it makes it hard to reach you. Many spirits are trying to get to you. You will have to be on guard, as to which ones to listen to. Sara and I will look out for you. You will make contact with many more spirits who will give you good honest information, so do not think that all spirits are bad. You are feeling better now that you know that it is a message from Sara and I, and not an evil spirit as you thought it might be.

Goodnight.

GEORGE: You are getting a number of messages, as you are getting deeper into the Spiritual world. You seem to have contact with a number of people that want to talk with you, but who are having trouble getting to you. The lady called Sara is a good person. You will talk to her many times, as she has a great interest in your future. She is giving you honest answers to what you have asked her. You will no longer have to worry about the future, as there will be spirits to guide you now. Only when it is necessary, will they let you know that they are here.

SARA: You are to have many Guides throughout your lifetime on earth. You have more than George and I now, however, you do not know of them as yet. They will make themselves known to you, as time goes by, but not soon.

SARA: Yes, I will speak to you often. However, you are not to be upset by anyone when we are talking as it cuts off our communication, and I cannot always get you back when this happens. Try to have them leave you alone when you are speaking to me, as I do not want to share your thoughts with anyone while we are talking. Peter is with us here. You have nothing to worry about. Yes, if you like, George will speak to you.

*It seemed, at this time, as though the spirit contact was reading my mind. This accounts for the answering of questions. A thought would come into my mind and it was as if I had asked it as a question by the manner in which they answered me in the writing

SPIRIT: Are you happy with the way things are going? You will be able to question us in the near future, as you are passing through a stage where we are trying your strength. You have done well by yourself. Now you must wait another few days to get to be able to ask questions from us.

December 10, 1979

SARA: Good morning Peter. You are going to find that I will want to talk to you anytime you want to talk. It is not necessary for you to talk to me in the morning only.

Question: *Why does George not talk to me?*

He is getting ready to talk to you, but he cannot seem to get through to you. You must speak to him, as though he was there with you. He wants to speak to you as he has many things to tell you.

Question: *Will he be a Guide?*

Yes, he will remain your Guide for some time, until others are chosen to replace him. Goodnight.

December 12, 1979

SPIRIT FRIEND: Will you open your mind and let me communicate with you? You are trying to talk to me, and I cannot reach out to you. Try to leave all other thoughts out of your mind. You can be a strong medium if you practice. Last time you talked to me, I told you we were friends many years ago. That was to give you some insight into your past incarnations. I will be telling you much more about your last lifetime very soon. Right now you must stop getting too upset with other problems and listen to what is in store for your future as it is much more important to you. You are to give me your undivided attention, as it is the only way we will be able to communicate with one another.

* *I was beginning to feel like a school kid who was having problems with his teacher. I found myself trying to understand this incredible thing that was happening to my life, and they wanted me to concentrate! I might add that it was already a "very busy life". With my management position, along with family, service club and a few other involvements, I was putting in some very long days already, and they were telling me I had to clear my mind. What had I gotten myself into?*

Question: *Will I speak with George soon?*

Yes, he is waiting to talk to you, but wants to have you call on him only when you are ready to accept what he has to say to you.

December 17, 1979

Question: *Will you answer a question please?*

SPIRIT FRIEND: I will answer whatever I can. Your mind is giving you the message before your hand can write it - it is nothing to worry about. I will take a look in on you tomorrow.

December 20, 1979

SPIRIT FRIEND: Your thoughts are all wrong. Try to get more mentally ready before you try writing. You are not prepared for my message.

As Told To Me

December 23, 1979

SPIRIT: I have given you messages a few times now; however, you are better not knowing whom they come from until you have spoken with your Guide. George will be speaking with you soon, and he will tell you who we are. As you have many Spiritual contacts, you will want to know whom you are talking to. Yes, you will be in contact with your friends on many occasions for many years to come. You are to have a chosen purpose to receive these messages. You will spread the word of some of the things you are told, as to bring further understanding to the people around you. As a chosen person, you have the necessary mission in life; you must fill it to the satisfaction of many. Do not be alarmed that you have been chosen for this, as you have led a good life and you have a good heart and feel strongly for your fellow man. Be of good faith my son, as he who is good unto others, shall have good unto him. As I have spoken, so shall it be.

At this point in time I was having a great deal of difficulty accepting what they were telling me. I did not feel at all prepared for this. I made up my mind I would try this for a while to see where it was going to take me.

December 24, 1979

SPIRIT: You are going to receive a message from the heavens from a messenger who will say unto you, "Go forth and spread the wisdom that you shall be given." He who seeeth me lives in everlasting glory. You will know who calls upon you, when the time draws near.

December 25, 1979

SPIRIT: On many occasions you have been called upon to make contact with members of the chosen few. You are in trouble with yourself as to whether you are receiving a genuine message.

December 27, 1979

SPIRIT: You are going to receive a message from a strong spirit who will help you to understand the problems you think you are having.

Question: *Will it be soon?*

Yes, it will be, as it is very important to you that you understand all that is being said to you. You are soon to be a truly great medium, and all will be yours. You will talk with many incarnates, and find many answers to many questions, questions that are bothering many people. You must seek out a fellow medium to clear your mind that all is true, and you are not making it up in your mind. All will clear, when the time is right.

Question: *Will I do trance writing?*

Yes you may find it fulfilling.

Question: *Will I speak to George again soon?*

Yes you will again speak to George, but only for a short time, as George is not versed in the telepathy that you are now getting into. Your cross with George was a very freak happening that does not always occur. You are to cross with many who will give you more information than George can.

December 28, 1979

SARA: Peter, you are going to have to keep reaching George, as he has many things to help you with. It has been awhile since we have spoken; however, you have many messages to receive and I do not want to block your chances to contact anyone.

*This was to be the beginning of my communication with "SARA". I was put at ease just making the connection with this very strong Spirit. From here on I felt more willing to try to follow the path that had opened before me. Sara was someone special. I hoped I could live up to her expectations.

Question: *Do you know who was contacting me the past few days?*

No, I do not know who has been in contact with you. However, heed well the words of the wise as you work to learn much about these matters in the future. You are progressing well at your writings. Stay at it. You will see it all clearer very soon. It is a gift that you have, and you must use it.

Question: *Will you contact me often?*

Yes, I will contact you many times.

Goodbye.

December 29, 1979

SPIRIT: You are not wrong tonight; you will go to sleep and see. Give us the chance to contact you, as you are ready for a much greater experience. You will have an out of body experience soon. This will better teach you the effects of the future. Everlasting life is here for one and all. It is the peace of mind and finding of it that is all-important.

You should try other forms of trance medium-ship as you have the special powers to do them. If you learn the secrets of faith, the following of God's message, then, as you speak, so others will speak. As you listen, so others will listen. Do not be afraid of the unknown, but look to it as a life hereafter that has the glory of God the Almighty as its strength. You will see forms of this afterlife when you have an out of body experience. Ask not of us, until you have seen me in another life.

You will have a great deal of work ahead of you as you journey to the edge of the Spiritual Universe. As you are enlightened, so shall you enlighten others. Be of faith in me, and I shall have faith in all that follow you.

You are mystified by your contact; however, there are many things the mind does not know of. You shall learn as others have before you. You may fear these messages, or, you may learn from them. You are gifted to learn, and you have made the contacts. It is you who has opened the door to another first life hereafter.

December 30, 1979

SPIRIT: Be of Good faith and you will walk with angels. Try to understand that you are being given a chance to look ahead of your life on earth. The books you are reading are of great help in clearing up many conceptions of an afterlife.

As you should be aware, we can communicate to you, therefore the mind and spirit never die, but go into stages of improvement of great magnitude over the earthbound body.

You are reading a copy of a book that leaves many questions in your mind. Find a copy of "God's Earth and My Heaven". It is a book that will tell you more of what you wish to know.

Note: *I have never pursued this; however, I have not forgotten.*

SPIRIT: Peter, you are receiving messages from many spirits. That is not a problem; however, you must know the good from the bad and we will tell you this. Asking my name will not help you now. You must get into trance medium-ship as soon as you can, as this is where you will get your greatest contacts. Try to get books on trance mediums from your library, as you will need help in getting into this in a more meaningful way.

You are not afraid of what is said; however, you do not know that what is said is being conveyed by a number of different spirits. Now you cannot clear whom you were talking to at any one time. With trance, you will be able to make a greater pure contact, as your own mind will be sleeping, and you will be possessed by the contacts you seek. I am not going to tell you now, but I will work with you in the future, as you have a great potential for teaching others that this world, following yours, is a place of all things of beauty. You must tell many of your experiences.

This was one of the many urgings to write this book. The bar was being raised continually. I wondered how I could keep up with the standards they had set for me. The suggestion of trance medium-ship is spoken of many times; however, I never felt that I needed it to channel their messages.

December 31, 1979

ART: A great many times you call, and I am giving you a message, but it does not always come to you as I have sent it. You are trying always to write what you thought was being sent, and sometimes get it down wrong. Try letting me do the wording. You are doing it now.

*At the beginning, I was confused by the way some messages would come to me. It was about this time that I began doubting myself about all this.

Peter, you are going to get lots of calls from a group that are working with you, as they have much to tell you. You will know who spirits are, by the messages you receive. Yes, they will give you a name.

Start by trying a meditation period before writing. You can try this at any time. You do not have to call on us at a certain time of the day. Meditate for an hour, if possible, to clear your mind of all questions you have, as this is the best way to be prepared to receive our messages. You are not second-guessing me, as you are only reading my thoughts that are for you.

Note: *You will notice that there are many dates not included in this book. Many of these messages are left out as they were of a personal nature, or they did not add anything meaningful to this book.*

You are getting better at getting into trance state. Keep up the practice, as it will be the only way that your mind will be free of thought when you call on us. There are others, who shall be known for their psychic work, and you have the ability to receive them from here. You are intrigued by the books you have read. That is good as long as it has opened your mind to receiving messages others would not be able to. Peter, you are going to change lifestyles very soon, as you will become known for your psychic ability.

In troubled times, the people who can tell what is about to happen, are sought after by many. Your name will soon come up as a crestfallen world looks to the knowledgeable ones for answers. You are not unknown to me, as I am to you. You have shared a lifetime with me in another incarnation. You were a leader then, and you will find you have influence over other people. Keep calling on me, let yourself go, and let my message flow through to you.

January 17, 1980

SPIRIT: Peter, you were thinking of an accident that you saw in your dreams. The road is swaying because of an earthquake that will happen. You may be involved from the way it looks in your dream; however, you will not be anywhere near a quake area. However, the quake will exist as you saw it.

Question: *Where will it happen?*

No, it is not for us to tell these things.

Question: *Can I reach George now?*

Yes, George is here and will be in contact again. He is very busy with his work. He is looking forward to another session with you now that you are more ready to receive him. Try writing in the evening to get him.

Goodbye.

January 18, 1980

ART: You are going to become a grandfather this year. Helping you to understand the life, after you leave your present life form, is going to become the job of the spirit you have never spoken with in your writings. He will bring you many thoughts that you will be able to see in your mind, as to what it will be like on this plane. You will have many years to prepare. You have been here many times; however, the mind controls all thoughts of that which is not something that should concern you now. However, it is never too early to begin to set your life at the tempo you wish to enter the spirit plane, and take your place in God's presence. You were not about to become a religious man; however, your spirit is clear on the tablet of life. You are going to become a godly man as time goes on. You have a gentle feeling for man's troubled ways. You were a man of great faith in past incarnations and it shows in your feeling toward the people you try to help. Your work with the service club is only a cover for the true feelings about your fellow man. You try to make the lifestyles of others more comfortable by working in your club. Getting to know your feelings will prepare you for this side.

Goodnight.

January 24, 1980

SPIRIT: You had a very good meeting last night; you should be ready for the first session in hypnosis at any time. You are going to meet with another person soon, who will hear about you from the meeting last night. You will see that it is a very special gift you have, to receive messages from the spirit world, and to be able to transform this into talking lessons. In performing trance hypnosis it will lead to other greater things. You will become more involved with your writings as well, if you practice self- hypnosis. It will free your mind and let your spirit roam, as you are not able to attempt to do now.

This was in reference to the meeting I had with the Parapsychologist. His encouragement meant a lot to my advancement with the writings, as at this time I was quite confused with it all. Meeting someone who had had a similar experience gave me a great deal more confidence to continue on with this writing.

Peter, you have not gotten through the learning process; however, you are learning well as you seek to understand what has been within your ability to grasp.

Start to take life as it comes to you. Many changes are to come as you have already been told. Put faith in the facts you have learned, and try to understand what happens so you will be ready. There are a few on your side, who are ready to accept as fact that which is about to unfold. The world has a coming tragic event that will not affect you or your family, as you are where you were to be. Do not labour on this, as you can have no effect on the outcome. So it is to be, so it shall be.

*Once again the message was not given a signature. This was to happen on many occasions during the first few months. However, I did not seem to sense a different spiritual contact on many of these occasions. The expectations for my future seemed unattainable to me.

January 25, 1980

SPIRIT: The gathering of clans does not mean the end is near. You are about to embark on a mission of responsibility that will give you insight into many things. Do not get too involved, as you will find you will inspire others to do some of the work for you. You will be able to get results from the endeavor you are thinking about. It is a noble thing you are doing for the kind people who are deserving of your help. A very keen interest is being placed on your performance of your duty to mankind. You serve him well. Will you try to help others in need for as long as need exists? Many forms of help will be suggested to you. Select the ones you feel will work for you. Doing God's work is why you are here. You're serving well. Do not let a few people worry you, as they mean well. However, do not have the instinct to do the work alone. It will work out well, as you have many friends who support your cause. Continue to find ways you may help others, as it is God's commandment to help the poor and the feeble of body as they too are from the kingdom of heaven.

This particular message may well have had a special meaning at the time, as I was involved with a project to assist the Salvation Army in replacing their badly worn old passenger van. The van needed extensive repair that well exceeded its value. I went shopping and located a newer van at a cost that the service club could afford. It was what I would refer to as a 'feel good' situation.

January 29, 1980

SPIRIT: We are all God's children; all are able to see and be seen in his presence. Do unto others as you would have them do unto you, so you will be a better soul. Part not your spirit from your Creator, as it is those who become complete who shall find total commitment with God. Try not to be of ill faith as ye so live this life, so shall ye be judged hereafter.

Yes your world will be shaken by a number of earthquakes, and there will be widespread bellows of heat that will annihilate many. It will happen, as it is meant to be, and as it is meant to be, so be it. This will not happen for many of your years yet; however, it could be set about by a misleading fool, who could set your world to warfare over atomic weapons. Many people will pass over when this traumatic time hits your planet.

All will not suffer this fate; however, he who likes to dominate shall himself be dominated by destruction. No, you will not suffer earthquakes where you are now, but you will not be without trouble. You will overcome these as you are a strong nation, and should be able to find ways to start yourselves back to a better way of life. Trust in God, and all who are to be saved shall see him only when it is time.

Go slowly, as you are not well. You may bring about a problem if you push too hard. You have seen a problem arise and have been aware of its presence. It will not be detected as a problem in time to stop it. Think and it will be obvious to you. No, it will not be fatal, as you are to be of further need and cannot be leaving what you have started. You are about to journey to a new experience. You will find it alarming at first; however, you will learn much of what you wish to know.

There are things you do not control, but you will not be left to fight them alone, as you have many who look out for you. You know that, as well as I do. It will not be feasible to postpone anything, as you will not be affected for that long. You will have to change your lifestyle, as you will not be able to work as hard as you presently are. One does not take from the fire a log and still receive the same heat.

As Told To Me

*This message, again, was meant for me in a personal way; however, I felt it contained a very good closing line and felt compelled to add it to the rest of this book. In regards to the reference to my heath, it was to do with a kidney problem I was having.

February 1, 1980

SARA: You are about to start a new year. It will hold many changes for you. A new enterprise may well be in store, as you well know, having spoken of this with a friend. No future fortune telling is done, however you have a set destiny and it will unfold in due time. Wise decisions are to be made and you should not find any problems in dealing with them.

Now for something else: you are not going to change your lifestyle a great deal, but you will have greater security in the near future. Destiny can be controlled. It is not all by chance. If it were, what shape would the world be in today, if man could not in some way shape his future? Look over your shoulder at what has passed before you. Do you not see the shaping of things in your past? So you will shape your future.

*One of the biggest changes in my lifestyle has been to find the time necessary to compile this book. But I must confess, when I look back over a period of many years, a lot of things would surely be different had I not taken the path that I did.

February 4, 1980.

Question: I have not heard from George for some time, will I contact him again?

Yes, it is going to happen; however, it will be in his time and it will be only as he decides.

Question: Will it be as strong a contact as we have had in the past?

Yes it shall, as George is a very forceful person. He will want to control the conversation.

Question: Should I be trying to get George at a different time of the day?

He will contact you in such a way you will have no doubt that he wishes to speak with you.

Question: if I was able to get involved with the séance would I be able to make voice contact with him?

You may well do, as you have many ways of contact that are to be shown to you yet.

*George did make contact with me. He also dominated the contact, as he spoke of each member in the family. As much of his message was on the personal side, I have not added it to this book.

February 5, 1980

SARA: Good morning, you want to know things that have happened to you in the past?

Well, you were a very strong person when you spent time on earth. You had a will to do many things, and you are gifted with the laws of gravitation, so that you were able to understand how birds flew. You were also studying the possibility of man flying.

Question: When was this?

It was 1791. You lived in a place in Denmark. You were a scholar and you were also a leading member of the Society for the preservation of wild things. Studies were your main course in life. As you were very wealthy you did not have to work for a living. Many a day was spent in deep contemplation on the state of the world around you. You were never able to convince the right people that a means of flight for man was possible. Be of special care as to whom you discuss your personal life with. Many do not have your insight to the hereafter, or of many matters they are afraid to speak of.

The reference to me living in Denmark was never followed up on.

February 6, 1980

SARA: Yes, you are wondering about your past lives. Well, you were a splendid example of what life on your side should have been. You were a God-fearing man, as they would say today. However, it was God loving and not fear that made your friends all think so highly of you. You made your way in the church and also as a sage going about the country preaching of the good that comes out of a life with God. Your family was not all of this strong belief. You did not stay at home and preach to them, as they shunned you as a God sent messenger that would keep them from going about the ways they had chosen for themselves. It was very hard for you to keep a long distance away, as you loved your family even though they shunned you. You lived off the land and were apt to get food and shelter from many that brought encouragement to you as you travelled about the country. Your wife left you and you never returned to your home for many years as you stayed in a monastery for many years doing your work for your Creator.

The story you are told is not a fable, but the way you lived in another lifetime. Be sure to understand that little of this can change your present way of life. You are gifted to be able to help others in that you care as to the well-being and comfort of others. This stems from your deep concern for mankind in your past incarnations. It is time we settled a few things about your present life. You are not a man of the cloth as you expected to be; however, you have been doing your job to make the lives of others a little easier as you work with the service club. This work is important to you, as it is an outlet for the many things you had wanted to do. There will come a time when this will not be enough for you and you will seek other ways to express yourself. Time changes the weather, as well as man's mind. You will find that you are closer to God than you think you are.

February 8, 1980

SARA: Peter, your past lives reflect a definite commitment to making life better for others. Although you were never a Spiritual leader, you worked more with the individual than with the masses. Try to look on it as someone who made their life better by giving feeling and guidance to others.

There are too few of this type of person today, as everyone is bound in their own thoughts and deeds. As a man who has been helpful to others before, it has come to you once again now as you are still trying to carry out the same lifestyle this time around. If you were to leave the club work, you'd be lost for a while until you were able to find a new outlet for this way you work with the less fortunate. All men are meant to take heed of their brother's plight, but all men do not try to assist. It is said that he who does the Lord's work, he too shall hear the Lord's praise. At a time when all mankind can no longer live in peace, it will take many worthy souls to try to bring mankind to the point of understanding. Those that have a better understanding of what is to come will have to lead the rest. There are many changes yet for your present world to go through before they will see the benefits to living as one. All will not be pleasant as "so goeth the wind in rage, so cometh the calm".

February 9, 1980

SARA: Peter, be of faith as you are chosen to be a leader. Your writings will be used for future research into the world hereafter, as it is sometimes referred to on your side. There are many things that will be told to you, that you must keep, so you will be able to assist others who also feel the draw of the spirit world. Try coming to the writing at an earlier time, so as to let us give you more of a message before you have to run off to work.

Question: Will you be relaying facts of the past?

Yes, we will; however, only as we feel it is justified in doing so.

Question: Meaning?

You will only be able to adjust to a certain amount of this at one time. Better we get you to a stage of understanding before we start to unload the history of time on you. All will happen when it is time. You have progressed rather well to the point you are at now, but it is still a long silver road you have to travel. When you get there, doors will open and the mind will take over all matters you cannot now understand.

Question: Will I write a book from this information you give me?

Not right away, but it will happen. Follow your feelings to get the proper perspective.

February 10, 1980

Question: Will I ever be told things that would allow me to write a book, and have it published about the life hereafter?

SARA: Yes, it is the reason for our concern in your life that you explain to others. Life after death is a more lovely existence than they can imagine. The book you are thinking about will be ready in a year or two; however, you will need more time to write it than you have now. Perhaps your sudden turn to wealth may give you the time you need. Do not shut the door when you have only come halfway in. I know you are sincere. You have qualities that are required to do this thing and see it through.

Question: When will we start on this book?

It will require a little more time spent on this until your mind is free of all business matters, to be able to get on with it. It will happen and you will have acquired a few more on this side to assist you by then. Others are now making time for you in their busy schedules. Your interest may be that which you do not now perceive; however, you are going to go in many different aspects of life to achieve the perfection you wish. "Go not into the dark, lest ye first light a candle."

*I'm still waiting for my "sudden turn to wealth."

February 11, 1980

SARA: Good morning Peter. I tried to get you up earlier but was not too successful; however, we will make the best of the time we have. Peter, about four years ago you saw a very large house on the lake and wondered who would have lived there. Well, I did. It was secluded by trees and it is so close to the water.

Question: What Lake was it on?

Lake Rosseau. It is about a mile and a half past the marina on the North Shore. Your boat passed by while I was contemplating a return to that area and I got interested in your life. You likely did not know that we are able to detect if someone is psychic. We do not make contact with everyone, only those that show a gift of receiving our messages. So, our lives crossed while you were there and I here.

February 12, 1980

SARA: Good morning Peter, you have tried to give me a little more time I see. Well, on to our story. You are aware that I have lived in the place you call Muskoka. It was not known as that when I lived in that area. At that time, it was merely Upper Canada and a long way from the civilized world. Things were not easy then, nor were they all bad, as the land had a beauty that was to be beholding. The lakes and rivers were crystal clear and the forests were mightier than now. So many changes after the passing of time, that all the things I cherished are now replaced with other spots of equal beauty. The river falls have changed very much, as has the location of the town you live in. You would be amazed at the number of people who lived there, while I lived on the upper lakes. It was a voyage of some undertaking to venture down by long boats to your site, while we were on the upper lakes. To go to the mouth of the river it would take a day's travel for us. You have it so much better now, getting to and fro in a few minutes time, although you miss a great deal of the beauty as you travel by so fast. Try to imagine rowing your boat to the tops of the lakes and what you would see on the way up. We also had to portage the falls at the Narrows you now call the lock. I would try to tell you how it was here at that time, however it is time you were away.

As Told To Me

February 13, 1980

SPIRIT: Good morning. Peter, Sara is not with us today, so we will give you something else. Do not worry about Sara. She will be back. She is helping out a new arrival. Sara was telling you of her past life and I think it would be best if she continued that herself. You don't mind, do you? Okay, so how be we talk about you a little today?

You have been reincarnated many times since the time spirits started to populate the world of yours. You have seen many lifestyles; however, your personality has changed little. You enjoy your time on earth, and have kept returning very quickly after each time you leave. It is sad that many spirits are trying to find themselves. You have found that life has always included many others. Your way with people comes from so many, many contacts you have made over the centuries. You are kindred with many of the ones you come in contact with. Others have followed your returns to be close to you again and, as God wishes, all who live together in harmony shall dwell in the sight of God. Sara shall be with you tomorrow, as she is near finished with her plight of others. She said to tell you she was sorry she could not be here, but some things do have to come first. This story Sara is telling you, should keep you guessing for a while, but it does have a bearing on your life as well.

That's all I can tell you about it for now, so keep on with our little talk. You will want to know many things about your past, better you take it as it comes to you. As you see, all is not available at a moment's notice. To give you that, let me explain that your records have to be checked. Just as you would check on someone there, it takes some time here as well. You will learn much from Sara, as she holds you dearly in her thoughts. You have been very close many times before. Well, must leave you now Peter, Godspeed.

February 14, 1980

SPIRIT: Good morning. You are about to receive a message from George. How do you think it will compare with that which Sara has been telling you? If it is not what you expect, do not let it get you down, as there are many things in store, and all will take time. On to the matter at hand. Peter, you want to know more of your past lives, as well as something about the future you are going to have. Well, fortune telling is not our game; however, it is possible to know through the thoughts of others that there are some changes in store for you and your family. You have served your karma well and your rewards are in heaven, as they say on your side. However, all do not wait that long. Things are about to start happening and your course in life will change. It will be for the better, with a little more time to relax and start a book maybe. Try to imagine yourself in a desert scene, as you will be visiting one. Does it bother you waiting for Sara? Of course it should not, as you would otherwise not have gotten to communicate with me.

Question: Can you tell me your name?

Not yet, but some time perhaps it will be relevant to our conversation. For now I will talk and you write while I look over your shoulder (at this time I turned not knowing what to expect). Did you expect to see me? Well, Peter, we are going to discuss your past lives; however, it has to be done systematically if possible. Where should we start?

The first time you showed up, looks like you were in Atlantis. While there you served as the master ship builder, and a knowledgeable person to be sure. You were married and had many children, some of whom are near you now. You were your own boss, so to speak, as it was left to you to build the ships that travel the world. Your ship-building was an art. Many times the Masters would ask that you join them in battle against many of the smaller nations, but you would not partake of the plundering that they condoned.

February 18, 1980

SARA: Yes Peter, I am here, we will get on with our story. I am glad you missed me; however, I do believe you did receive a very strong message from the spirits who waited on your call. As I was saying before we parted, I once lived near you. It was a different land then. You could not find a cottage for many miles along the shore. My father was a trapper and he would travel the lakes and rivers looking for beaver and raccoon. Wildlife was very bountiful in those days, so it was not hard to get a large catch. Then there was a long journey to the fort of York to try and sell the furs. Your father's grandfather was also a trapper at one time; however, he was hurt and lay dying in the bush. When he was found he returned to England, as it was his home.

Your thoughts are not clear this morning Peter. You cannot concentrate. Let's try tomorrow. Go, as you would return, as you will.

February 19, 1980

SARA: Try to imagine a mountain that is a desert scene. This will give you some idea of what it may be like after the next cataclysm. You will be spared, as will many of yours. However, things will change drastically. Your weather will turn tropic and the seas will be warm on your shores. It will happen sooner than many realize. Do not fear the shifting as it will only be felt by the ones who do not fit into God's creation of a complete world. Many things will happen to change the lives of many people; however, it will take a long time to settle into the way things are to be.

Few will be ready for this change, as the scientists of your time will not believe it. Nor are there many who believe this to be happening but it shall happen, and you will remain in your contact with us. Much will be said afterwards as to who could have predicted it, but only a few, such as you, will be able to look back and say "there are notes where I was told of such a thing." This is not a morbid thing, as God will cleanse the earth of many who refuse to live up to his rule. Love thy brother as you would love thy God. We cannot tell you when it will happen, only that it is inevitable. Do not try to explain to others who do not wish to listen of it. All will witness the power that only God can create. When many lands slip into the sea and once again Atlantis rises from the deep, so shall the ones remaining believe in God, as the lost records of mankind shall be brought forth from the depth of Atlantis for all to see. Trust not the judgment of others, but stay fast where you are, and no harm will come to you. Love is everlasting, so is thy God.

As Told To Me

February 20, 1980

SARA: Peter, do you have the courage to continue our messages, as you may find out things about yourself you do not like, or find hard to associate with? It should not bother you too much, as you are strong of heart and soul. To have lived through the various lifestyles you have lived, you must have been a hardy spirit.

Your past lives include time when you were a prisoner of the damned. You were a rustler and a thief in the days of old Egypt. When you were caught, you killed the guards and escaped to the far eastern shores of the Asian world and became a man of wealth. No one found you out, but when your life was over, you had to pay karma to atone for your misdeeds in the flesh. You returned almost immediately, as you were never one to stay on here very long.

The next time on earth, you came back as a beggar. You lost a leg and one hand at sea, and were not able to get around that well. Hardship was your way of life as you lived from day to day, never having a roof above you, lest you were able to find shelter in a stranger's loft. Life was extremely hard on you as often you were robbed by thieves who would then torture you, and steal the money you had begged for. You paid your karma well with that life.

February 21, 1980

SARA: The day is short now. Did you sleep in? Okay, it is still time enough to give you a few moments. When you were a young man in a previous life, you saved someone from drowning. That person is with you now. Peter, you have a past that is quite full of meaningful happenings. When you refused to give of your life on earth, you set aside a chance to progress on this side. You were ready, but you wanted to be near the ones you came to love on earth. Each time you returned, someone was there with you from a previous life. Your wife has been with you twice before, once as your wife and once as a sister to you. You see, it is possible to remain forever with the ones you love, if you follow into the next incarnation. Life is everlasting, only you must use it wisely, as your sole purpose is that of becoming a complete and cleansed spirit. Perfection is there for all to attain; failure is there for those who do not try.

February 22, 1980

SPIRIT: We want you to go into a deeper trance, so as to ensure a greater pull between us. You are getting good enough at it that you should be able to induce a hypnotic trance state. Try this when you have more time. You may want to try in the evening, when you do not have to leave so quickly. The deeper the trance, the better it is to receive some of the higher messages. You have come a long way since we first started. It is necessary to give you a rather abrupt start, with little control on your end to get you started. If you sat there and nothing happened, you would not be receiving as you are today. However, all things must progress and it's getting time for you to try something still more enlightening. If you can induce self hypnosis, you will be in a more direct contact than you ever hoped to be. Many things will come to you then. Start by doing your exercises and then try the deep breathing exercise. Concentrate on the clear blue sky. As you start to go under, you will see colors and the feeling of weightlessness will be with you. Have no fear. You will not be alone as there will be someone ready to bring you out of it, if you wish. This will start a new series of information. You may wish to progress then into speaking with the spirits of others, such as many other mediums do. It will be easy for you to get into this as you are learning fast now. Try to look at it as a book that you do not have time to read and someone is reading it to you. Many things will come from this. Your spirit will be stronger and you will help others to communicate with loved ones who have passed over. Your reception is good now, but under trance you will be even better as the Spirit is there unaware of happenings around you. This way, you can concentrate on hearing only the voice that you wish. This is telepathic communication. Sara is not with us today.

February 24, 1980

SPIRIT: What you hear is not what you will see. All things are not as you see either. Do not go into the world looking for the answers of mankind, as the answers lie not in yourself, but in the glory of God. Only He has the answers and the cures for mankind. Try to imagine keeping millions of souls free of ills and want. It is a fantastic thing to conceive. However, if man were to return to his original state, he would no longer suffer the fate of mankind today. Illness is man's creation, not that of our Creator. Let mankind return to the life of purity, and salvation will be his. Let him continue as he is, and man will continue to suffer his own ill begotten ways. Go not into the land with your eyes shut, as you are never to see the glory of God's creation. Let not that you go with eyes closed to his temple, and see not his healing ways. Let your feelings come through, as would a baby cry for its nourishment. "For I shall hear all", said the Creator, and try not to stifle the sound as the spirit need shall be fulfilled. Yea, thou are the son and daughter of God, and he that puts the Lord thy God on high, shall glory in the light of God forever. Be of faith, for faith only is thy tomorrow. God be with you.

I do believe the entry on this date is one that will be read over a number of times. There is a very deep message contained here and I do hope that my readers take the time to explore the meaning of the message. It speaks loudly to me, but you may find your own interpretation. I feel this was channelled this way to make the reader think carefully about what they have read.

February 25, 1980

SARA: Peter, you are not trying to trance state yourself. Don't be afraid of it, I will help you. The results will be gratifying to you, for as you learn more about it, you will be able to go from one state to another with little effort. It's like taking a trip to a different part of the country you have never seen. There will be no ill effects on you, as you are under our constant care. Try tonight if you like. I know you want to have things just right to try it, but you will get results. When you are under, you may want to speak with someone on this side, so have someone ready to take notes. Your keeping these books will be of great help to you sometime. You are not thinking of trying to keep up the session this morning as you are wandering in your mind. Try to reach me tonight.

February 26, 1980

SARA: Where were you last night? We had hoped to try the trance. Okay Peter, I understand you are also working under great pressure these days as well, so it is understandable that you are tired and not up to it. When you are ready I will help you. You should try a holiday in warmer weather. You will be able to; it's not that far off. Things are going to change and you will travel. You will want to see some of the old ruins of your ancient past. It is this way you will come to understand more of the things we tell you. Egypt will enter into our story and you must see it to remember your past. Some do not remember; however, you are chosen to be one who will relate to others the glory that once reigned supreme. What we tell you must be used in a way that all who wish to believe, will have not a moment's hesitation, when they hear you speak or read your lectures. If it takes financial rewards to free you of your time it will come about, as so you have been chosen, so you shall proceed. It all will take time, as time is your biggest problem now. We must have more of it, to better equip you for your travels.

A strong reference to Egypt was made at this time; however, it hasn't happened (yet).

February 27, 1980

SARA: Peter, please try to get time to do what we suggested to you. It will open a new awareness to you. Your mind should be ready now for us to communicate more thoroughly. Do your exercises first and then try letting yourself float. Your mind will be clearer and you will find this new way much more meaningful, as you will have voice contact with many of the spirit world. Few mortals are given this chance at communicating with us Peter, so please do not put it off. I know you have been busy, but it's very important that we get on with this soon. Put all other things aside and give this a try tonight, but also do not be alarmed if you have some difficulty at first getting through, as it's a new step in a total communication of life. Few things that happen will ever surpass the presence of communication with the spirit of someone you have known, or someone whom you have never heard of, but who wants to relay a message to your world. You are to become a trance medium. You are impressed by some books you have read and this is how you have been chosen to come into the new field of spirit communication. It will take time to perfect your trance; however, you have the group on this side working with you, so all should go very smoothly. A new world awaits you and a challenge you would never have thought existed before. As new things take time, you will need patience, as you have done with your writings. By the way, we do not want you to stop the writings but to carry on as well.

February 28, 1980

SPIRIT: Time is an element of man. None has the patience for it to take its allotted cycle to begin and end. As the universe unfolds, you find that time has held the entire world at its mercy. You go by the clock to rise in the morning as you do to retire at night. If all mankind were to leave their clocks alone for one week, what a difference it would make. Did you ever think what would happen if you did not set your time to complete things, that many would be done in a better way? The pressure of rushing here and there is common to you, but it was never set up to be this way. Days were set into light, night into darkness. The rest of the time was twilight and dusk. Would man not do well to settle for a less hectic pace and fit his living and his work into a time spell that would serve him better?

February 29, 1980

SPIRIT: Your friends will look upon the things you are doing as rather strange. You are aware of this, we are sure; however, you have a way of overcoming a problem, so onward and upward as you say. You go through life as a guide of time, always at its beck and call. The true meaning of time leaves one without any idea of why it was broken into such minutes and seconds. Time is the passing of space. You all live in a cycle of space. Without it, no man shall move beyond where he stands.

March 2, 1980

SARA: Were you hoping to find someone at this time of day? Well, I held out for you, as you are usually a late riser on Sunday morning. Things are about to happen as we have told you. This is going to have quite an effect on your life at first. Be careful to heed directions; you do not want to become a person whom you are not. Many ideas have been transferred to you in thought pattern and this should help you decide what you should do. You have chosen the road you wish to take and you cannot go back on it. It's like the yellow brick road; it will lead you to whatever you wish; however, you could also get hopelessly lost on it as well. We know you will make the right decisions as you have a past history of being a very humanitarian person. You have friends who can use the help, as well as strangers. Treat every matter with great deliberation, as your decisions have to be the right ones. Time will prove you to be the benefactor to many needy people. The time is near to see yourself as a very prominent person in many ways. The fate of mankind is set. You can only alter that which is possible now. Go with the word of God as you make your way through the times ahead of you. Your fellow man is in for many changes as we near the catastrophe of another world holocaust. The day the axis shifts will separate many lands and the sea will divulge many secrets. Atlantis will once again be there for all to see. You may also wish to return there.

Go with God

March 4, 1980

SPIRIT: As you go, so goeth the Lord. Do unto others as you would unto God. As you go, so go with your family, give to them as you would unto your God. As you go, so your children will follow. Be on the right path, as never do we walk the same path again. As you enter into the kingdom of glory you will meet thy son and all will be holy as he is a good spirit and awaits your return. Time is the measure of mankind and when time runs out the universe opens its doors to you. The way shall be lit for you as no one walks in darkness. Give to others the help you can now, as all mankind must return to start again on the quest for perfection. Your path has been lit, follow it well. Time is of no bearing on perfection. To some, 100 years is forever. To others, two score is too many. Trust that you shall have a greater duty to perform when you return here. Though your coming will bring great joy to many here, it will bring great sorrow to many there. Time is not measured here but drifts into eternity as all souls shall meet and depart again and again. God be at the side of your every move. So shall it be.

March 5, 1980

SPIRIT: Your goal will be fulfilled very soon. Remove all matters that distress you from your mind. The storm of time is not going to leave a mark on your life. Life is the golden rule. It will shine only when the proper measure of love is given in return for all that one receives. The Universe is full of glorious things to behold; however, very few get to accept them until they no longer can see them shine. The heavens open to a starlit sky, as one might observe the coming and going of Angels. The stars are there only to be seen at night but, as one man sleeps, another awakens to the light of day. This is the time when all men should pray for the salvation of the Universe. As God has set his staff, so shall the way be clear.

Question: And where is Sara this morning?

She is with the newcomers who need her guidance. She will return soon.

Here too I have felt the presence of another guide, and the absence of Sara. This may seem strange to you; however, to me it was like picking up the phone and hearing a strange voice. It's hard to explain it properly as I do not know the answers myself.

March 7, 1980

SPIRIT: You are going to be able to do many of the things you wish as time goes on. Travel is one of them you will enjoy very much. There are many things to see around the world, and many things more to see, if they ever find the hiding places of some. Yes, we know of some things that were hidden to protect the history of mankind, and somehow, they will be read by mankind again. The fact that all cannot be explained by mankind does not mean there is no explanation for its being. Wonders abound throughout the universe that defied mankind; however, we must never forget that there is a much higher being than mankind. As time unfolds, the wisdom of the universe shall come to the light of many who follow the path to God through his word. Let not that he walk in blindness. Have faith that all mankind will see the same light on his return.

March 8, 1980

LLOYD, the Traveler: An unusual conversation:

Good afternoon. Are you going to be calling on someone in the afternoon now? Don't be surprised to get someone other than Sara on these times, as she's not available now. Would you like to talk with me? My name is Lloyd; however, I am known as the 'Traveler' to my fellow spirits as I have been into more lifetimes on Earth than any of them. You have never met me in your present lifetime; however, you did ride with me in the old West. You see, you make many returns yourself.

Question: When did I ride with you?

It was '93 we rode together.

Question: Was it 1893?

Well it wasn't 1793! You wanted to be a lawman, but they didn't want you. Something about you shooting some man in Alabama. You shot a guy beating a black and they wanted you down there. Seems as though you were against a black getting beat on and you shot the bastard that was whooping him.

Question: What was my name then?

You was a Younger then, the name of Jessie. Not of the gang of bank robbers though, just the same last name. Maybe your brother's kids were the bad ones. Never did get in the law, but helped them out a few times though. Never thought you had the stuff to up and shoot a man, but guessing you did, cuz some of these Yankee bastards came a'lookin for you. You was wanted for another thing down that way. You shot two of the Yankees and the rest took off to Alabamy as I heard it. Still tried to get in with the law again this time I see; well, maybe they just don't like you, Jess. Seems we was always loners anyway. Man's got to protect what's hissin though. No tellin' who's going to steal your teeth now a day. Them was good times then."

Question: Where did we ride together?

We was in Kansas, Albuquerque, and was in Alberta and the north/west; anywhere there was a little work, a woman and a bottle of booze.

Question: Can you name a town in Alberta where we worked?

Sure, we was in Grand Forks for a couple of years, around '92. You sure was a hopping son of a gun in those days. Been wanting to go back, sure wishin' I could. Seems you're tamed down a might this time round. You sure ain't givin' them hell like you used to.

Try getting to me again, got lots more to tell you.

* The above 'conversation' with Lloyd was the only one that occurred with this rather different spirit. I included it to show how various in nature spirit contacts can be. On this same date George once again contacted me. I will not include his message as it was purely personal. It was, however, good to connect with him again.

March 9, 1980

SARA: Good morning. You are a late riser again today. Well, it's all right, as I knew you would make it. How did you enjoy your talk with George? He will get back to you another time. The group who talks with you are concerned that you take proper care of yourself as you are a very important link to us. Not many people have your gift of receiving our thoughts and you are also a great deal more interested than many others. You would like to write something literary, significant; however, this takes time, Peter and you are right by keeping all your notes. Someday, these will be of help to you and others as you progress through this lifetime.

Question: Will you tell me more about yourself Sara? I would like to know where you lived and when.

You will get all this in time Peter. You are going to want some information about other things as well. All will be brought to you at one time or other. My connection to you is not through family, but as someone you befriended along the way. Your past life on earth, as well as many before, will give you some bearing on the type of spirit you possess.

March 10, 1980

SARA: I hope that nothing interrupts our sessions. To have come this far, we certainly do not want to stop now. Do you find our sessions worthwhile? (I answered "yes".) That is good, as we have to be sure that you are getting something out of them. Your progress has been good. You learn fast, as you have picked up from the first forceful session with George, to your present state, where you are reading our thoughts. That is how it should be. It should not be necessary to be as forceful as George was, except to get you started. Well, go on with your writing wherever it is possible, as many things will come to light for you. Never was there a time for informing people as there is now. You can serve a great need to a number of others by putting them in touch with the spirit world. You will some day be doing trance hypnosis and through this you will speak with the spirits, as many mediums do. All will come in due time. For now be content, if you will, with talking with me and a few that fill in for me.

March 11, 1980

SPIRIT: Good morning Peter. Are you wondering about your medical test today? I cannot tell you for sure what they will find, but you will have to return for more, as it will not be conclusive from these that all is well. Do not let it bother you though, as all will come out okay in the end. You have nothing to fear, as you are watched over by an Angel of Mercy that will intervene when it is necessary. Down through the ages you have had some type of medical problem, only this time you feel it is the first. Memory of past lives will not bring you the suffering you have had.

March 12, 1980

SPIRIT: Good morning. Well, where do we start today? The story you wish to hear about the creation of time is not ready to be unfolded to you. However, in due time it will be told along with many other tales of the beginning. For now, you will have to be content with the things that we can bring to you.

March 13, 1980

SARA: My, you are a little late today. Well, not too much we can get in today. You were not going to forget to call on us though, that's good. Try to call even if you only have a minute of time, as it shows you do expect to find us here.

March 20, 1980

Question: Is there anything that can be done about ringing in the ears? Can you find me the answer?

SPIRIT: Yes, there is a cure for this as was suggested to you. Hypnosis would be very helpful as it is a way to have the body cure itself. No drugs are necessary. Try to find a doctor that specializes in hypnotic treatment. You will have to go to the big cities to find one; however, there are many who know how to treat the body's ills by the manipulation of the mind. After all, it is the mind that lets you sense the problem. It is also the mind that can cure it. You should try to relax by using head and neck exercises and by using a cold compress at the base of the neck right after the head exercises. A doctor of the art of hypnosis would alert you to the problem, then advise you that if you were to forget about it, it would slowly disappear through hypnotic suggestion. This will work. You should not be sceptical about it, just go and get on with it. Check for a doctor who uses hypnosis, as this is noted to be the best cure for many of mankind ills. Don't wait much longer as you are wasting many days you could enjoy, by having this ringing going on in your head. Use the information to your advantage. This is the real reason we communicate, to offer help.

March 21, 1980

SPIRIT: Be of good faith, and your health is going to improve. You must try to let your thoughts dwell on the righteous things of the Universe, as so you go with God in your heart, so God will come to you with salvation in his. For whosoever goeth with God walks not alone, but walks with God in all his glory. The rain and sun both shine for a different purpose, one to grow and one to nourish. Mankind is nourished by the light of God. All mankind will someday be a part once more of our total. All will be a part of one. Go not to arrive, but for the journey and its rewards.

April 2, 1980

SPIRIT: Don't think of death as a sad thing, for you know that the spirit lives on in glory. Try to look at life as a road to better things. Once we have passed down the road, it's only one leg of our journey. Don't let death deter you from living, as the goals must be met by doing both. Go and remember that all things shall come to pass, and all things shall end. The ending of one life is but a pause before the beginning of another. So it shall be that all life is eternal.

April 11, 1980

LUKE: The day draws near when all mankind shall unite once more. So as the tree is bent, so shall the roots take shape. Man was to walk straight, but he has bent. So shall he walk straight again. A tall tree casts a large shadow, a bush not but a glow does it change. All mankind should be tall. The day of redemption is near at hand for those who bend with no wind, but the strong of spirit will weather the pursuing storm. God be with you.

April 12, 1980

SPIRIT: When will you go away from here as a better man? All mankind must go on to a greater existence that will allow for a space of time to elapse. Your time allowed is measured not by years but by deeds. Perform them well and ye shall not labour in the darkness too long, for it is glory and the light of God that all mankind try to strive for. Let not the sudden passing upset the remaining few, as when one has achieved his goal, so shall he return to Heaven.

April 14, 1980

SPIRIT: We can all be as true to God's will as we want to be. Some may fall behind by giving in to their own illusions. What is about to be is about to be. Only God has the power to change man's destiny. Let that which is done in jest be forgiven, but that which is done in hate must be asked forgiveness for and repented for. No man walks higher than God, no man will be denied his mercy. As the tides turn, so shall events unfold. Mankind will live in peace when man learns to live with himself. Go forth and live the life of peace, but do not let the darkest night set back the light of day. Whosoever liveth by the rule shall pass on to the glory of the Hereafter, but those that destroy the peace shall languish in the depths of depression for penitence.

April 22, 1980

Question: Can I move objects with my mind only?

SARA: You may be able to do these things with a little practice. You have to direct your concentration to the object until you can picture only it in your mind. Strange things may be accomplished by the power of the mind. You should be able to do these things as you are gifted with stronger power than you have ever put to use. This writing is a good example. You never thought you would be able to do it; however, your progress is very good. New things happen as you direct your mind to the task. Never before have so few of mankind been adept in the reading of another's mind as now. Words need never be spoken if you have the insight of another's thoughts. The leaders of each nation should have these powers instead of nuclear power. It would do them far more good.

April 25, 1980

LUKE: Open your mind to the thoughts of ancient times. Many secrets lie in the old sayings and deeds of past civilizations. Someday, these will be found in the vicinity of the great pyramid. Others will come to light after the next great holocaust. Don't ever let the learned people of the day make you think they know all, as so little is known by the present civilization of this planet earth that it would be such as a pebble in the sand of the ocean floor. Mankind will never know all the answers until such time as life as you know it is no longer necessary. However, this could well be hundreds of thousands of years by your time before mankind is in probable and knowledgeable advancement for this to come about. Man's advancement is slow; it has to be. Otherwise, why would it be necessary to have the learning system? Without it, man would return to hunting with the beast of prey. Knowledge is the foundation of stability. To mankind, it gives a goal and objectives along the way. All people are created equal in the eyes of God, but not in the sight of man. To endure and succeed is the goal of God for all mankind.

You are not going to be able to move objects yet for awhile. That is done with total concentration. You will possibly do it at a later time. For now you have too much on your mind to give it the total concentration. You're giving much of your time to thought, but only when time is in less demand for you will you find success with new experiments. Keep up the interest; it will be fulfilled. You are now at a crossroad in life. What you do will determine how long it will last. Your previous life cycles on earth have never been for long durations. You have an illness undetected and it will not show for at least another year; then your faith will be tried. Do not sit idly by, but draw strength to the Spirit as that is the thing that brings one through any adversity. Live with tomorrow in mind, but do not dread life as it comes to you. You have chosen this life to live, and you must even the balance for a past life. All life is a trial to achieve the greatness needed to proceed to another hereafter of oneness with the creator of all life.

* Around this date there was interest in using the power of the mind to move objects. A TV show had someone bending silverware just using the mind.

April 26, 1980

LUKE: Hear the draw of the last breath. It is happening to someone close very soon. Draw strength from the soul as you are needed to carry out your duties. One must pass through the adversities of life to attain fulfillment of the spirit. As you go about your life, so goes the spirit on its quest for perfection. Life is not a beginning and an end. It is merely another cycle in our quest for perfection in the eyes of the Creator. When perfection is reached, no longer shall we endure life in the flesh. So complete will our spirit be that we will no longer wish to return to the body that is earthbound. We will live on in spirit forever in harmony with God. So it shall be that one and the same shall be the same. All unto God's will, we reach to the heavens as that is the final door.

*One cannot live without feeling the loss of someone's passing. It is much harder to accept when it is someone close to you.

April 30, 1980

LUKE: Only you can see the problems within your eternal soul. Once you have let your feelings rule your mind you no longer have control of the true spirit. Have your thoughts, but do not try to perform them as they are but an extension of the human feeling. The true feeling for anyone is felt within both at the same time. Only through a strong feeling of righteousness does one open his heart to God. While on the earth plane, one must learn to attune to many different temptations of love. The true love between man and woman was made of God's love for all.

April 30, 1980

SARA: You are still keeping a good schedule for us to get together. That is good, as only as we gain confidence in you, can we indulge in more specific topics. Your morning sessions are a good way to start the day. Listen well to what is said and you can only gain by it. The session should be kept to a definite time from now on, as you are working well at it. Your questions will soon be answered for you as you ask them. You have been wondering about the possibilities of other supernatural powers. Everyone has them. It is only a few who are able to claim them as a routine thing. If you try very hard, in complete concentration, you will do many things that others only read about. The power comes from the spirit. Many thousands of years ago, man used these powers to perform what are now called miracles; however, he merely used a God-given power that separated man from beast. The spirit lives on from one life to another but with little or no use, the powers of the mind are dormant, waiting to be called to act. Your mind is awakening to a completely different type of thinking and acting. Try some concentrated efforts to objects that are near you; the results will amaze you. It won't happen right away, as you may have to try many times to achieve what you desire. It will happen and you will then know of some of the mysteries of life that have eluded man for many centuries. Use the powers cautiously as they are but a gift and gifts can be broken.

May 6, 1980

SPIRIT: You have been chosen to accept the word of God. Try not that thy understand all, but grasp on to that which bringeth the greatest pleasure to the soul. Do as you would expect and that which is expected of you. Another day will bring you closer to the glory of God. Be not what you are, but what thy God wishes of you. The glory of God shall shine on those who help others. That which is written as the word of God shall no man take in vain, as he that walks with God shall never be without a companion. What greater company than to walk with thy maker, for as God commandeth so shall ye go. Not the light of day or the blackness of night can consume the shining light of the Lord thy God. When one walks alone he walks in torment of the things that trouble him to his grave, but to walk in the company of God, so the light of day will show the beauty of the universe and the dark of night will bring a restful peace. As you walk, walk with me, for as I go so shall ye go and when I rest so shall ye rest. "So Sayeth our Lord".

May 7, 1980

A FRIEND: Let go of your binding and journey to a distant place. There you will find peace of mind and contentment for the soul. Try not that you must succeed for the sake of success but succeed for the love of God.

As Told To Me

May 8, 1980

SPIRIT: Help not those who do not need it, but help those who need it and ask not. Open the path to glory as you go. No man stands alone, excepting he who has lost all faith.

May 13, 1980

SARA: Yes, you see a vision, but it's in the future, not your past. Someday you will remember seeing the rows of trees and you shall remember today. All things we envision are not real to us, but many are reflections of our lives. You are thinking ahead of me again Peter; let me tell the story. As I was saying, you may well have visited that tree lined lane, or road, but not in this lifetime. It can be a reflection of many lifetimes in the past. If the terrain does not look familiar then you have been there, but as someone else. Only the spirit could have remembered seeing it before, as the spirit lives forever.

May 14, 1980

SARA: Expand your existence and you will get more out of life. It is known that man cannot live by bread alone and his mind also must have a chance to challenge the knowledge he possesses. Through the open window we often see more than through a streaky pane. When a change in life is due, you must prepare for it.

June 13, 1980

SPIRIT: We are not going to be able to tell you much today, as many of your contacts are disposed in other activities.

You are not to worry, as Sara will be back soon. If possible you should meditate and reflect on previous conversations. Much can be learned from the notes you keep; read them thoroughly. When many such readings are put together, a strong influence is often present. But the thoughts and prayers of others help to keep you in understanding and acceptance of the contacts you have with this side. Few mortals ever get to where you are, as the fear of the unknown and fear of ridicule stop them from even thinking of the possibility that they may communicate with the past. You have reached a plateau that few people do. Expand on it and use it to guide your life. As no man can control his own destiny, at least you have the chance to know that there are options to be had. Trust in what you receive as you have reached a tide that will carry you over many hurdles. But, use your knowledge well, for he who fools others will he himself be proclaimed the fool.

June 17, 1980

SARA: You are still trying to get the answers to your past, I see. Well, perhaps I may be able to help you. Your past is something that may scare you and delight you at times. However, it's not all bad nor is it all good. We live these lives for the purpose of gaining grace with God, and sometimes we must lose grace to gain it sometime later. Your lives have been filled with a great deal of human suffering in the past, as you seldom lived beyond your 50th year and sometimes much less. The spiritual arrival that was to guide your existence is something you have sought inwardly for many years, and through many incarnations.

You are closer this time to reaching some of your goals than you have ever been. Comfortable as it may seem, you have many hurdles ahead of you to achieve your chosen position. Try to live life as it comes to you, as it is growing shorter each day. Not all shall receive three score and ten, for as the clocks wind down, so do we, as we reach the end of another cycle of learning. Your friends can attest to this, as you sometimes wonder why someone is left to attain while others are taken early. The days of reckoning are always just around the next bend. However, sometimes we are able to straighten out the road before we reach the bend. Your past has been one of a great deal of suffering at the hands of others, but this is over now, as you have chosen to be a different type of person this time and your debt is paid for the things you acted out before. Our purpose is to gain grace with God as we ascend the ladder of perfection to the oneness of the Universe. So shall it be that God and only God shall have dominion over our lives. It's with the grace of God that we returned to the flesh to gain yet another step on the ladder.

June 20, 1980

SARA: Very few are gifted with psychic power. The way you use it will determine how much you may get. It's a gift of knowledge from beyond the stars, as he who answers has traveled the galaxy of time and space. The true meanings of life are not learned while in the state of body, but are learned in the conscious mind when released from the bonds of the flesh. Much has been said of the hereafter; however, it is not to be seen as the hereafter, but as the present. For you see, you are not alive, then die and go to heaven, but you are here and have only returned to earth as you might visit a friend. You will return here and once again embrace the endless space of time in the presence of the Creator. It is not you that passes on, but the rest that stay a little longer. All shall return in time, but some shall go to earth again and again, wishing to find the total life, which is there for you to find. When you have found the answers you shall return, as is the rule. No man is God, but God is all mankind. Spend your time well, as you shall account for it well.

June 24, 1980

SARA: You may have to move on to another stage of the writing if your interest gives in. The facts that you would like are not about to happen so soon. You are new at this. Others are happy to be this far after years of practice. Someday the facts of living nature may be yours, but not until the time is right. Your mind is so tight with thoughts at all times that you have little time to expand on this. The little time you allow yourself is not sufficient to advance too fast. However, stay with it regardless of what others say. You are doing the right thing.

June 30, 1980

SPIRIT: Only you can please the ones that rely on you. Your sense of time is always at odds with others. You have the ability to understand; however, you do not always show it. Be sure you want what you are after as, when you get it, you will have to know how to use it. You must stay in touch with the spirit world, as all things originated in the minds of people who lived and who passed over. It's their thoughts that are transferred to deed on your side.

July 4, 1980

SARA: The way we look at life is the way we live it. When it's over you will not have the chance to change it. Only while you are living will you bring about these changes to sum up a better total for your karma. To live and not have atoned for a past life is a lifetime wasted. For he who has lost before shall never walk in total glory until he has cleared his soul of past sins against God and his fellow man. The debts are paid only when the deeds are done. Go onto the lands and bring love to all, as He would have it. All mankind needs to hear as God's law must be obeyed. Only he who enters the kingdom of heaven with the cleansed soul shall find the peace he pursues.

July 15, 1980

Question: Things have been said concerning my possible healing abilities. Will I someday be able to use this gift to help others?

SARA: Yes, you are going to learn of this healing art very soon. Fate has put you in touch with the people you now are acquainted with. They will help you to perform some very startling events that will lead you to being able to put your hands on others and use the powers you possess to heal their ills. Be of great caution; charlatans and fakes from other areas will hear of you and try to discredit you. However, when someone very prominent is healed by your powers you will then take your place beside your God and mankind. For whosoever gives of himself so shall God our Father give of Himself. Your path is clearing and the way will become clearer to you as you have a gift of God, and, as always, there is a reason and it is about to unfold.

July 16, 1980

Question: Sara, are you my guardian angel?

SARA: Yes, Peter I guess you could call it that. I am your Spirit Guide, who will be with you always. Are you pleased? The Guide's duty is to protect body and soul of the living. You have much to do as your life leads on to the final ending. I am here to assist you.

Question: Will you ever appear to me in a vision so that I might see what you look like?

I have, but you were not aware that it was not someone mortal. Someday it will happen as you wish it to. You will look up and see me standing there.

Question: Are you aware that the woman in my circle (close friends who gathered to practice) saw you when I was writing for them?

Yes, she asked that I appear, and by doing so it helped them to accept your gift of communication. She is a very spiritual woman and she is very interested in your power.

Although I'm now aware of having seen Sara, could it possibly be that she has appeared to me in a dream and I haven't recognized her?

July 18, 1980

SARA: We cannot tell what is to happen, but what will inevitably happen is set by the standards you live by. If you give of yourself, you shall receive likewise. If you share nothing, you shall find the loneliness of man without man. As the time of life slips by, so does the cycle of being with God get nearer. You must tell your story when the time comes, so that others may see the light of day from the darkness they share.

Question: Is it meant to be that I should attend the circle that is planned for Saturday night?

Yes, it is all starting to come together now. Your strength shall be tested before all. Fear not as you are as they see you. Your many strengths will be tried, and you shall take your place amongst the chosen. Give of yourself at this time, and be prepared for something that may amaze you; however, it is just another step in your journey. As so, you must complete your mission in this life.

Question: Is it possible that I will be able to help the sick and lame to find a cure as has been suggested to me?

As you continue you will cure many. This will start with the circle. You have been waited for; your appearance here has been expected. Do not expect to help all, as only the faithful may seek help to remain awhile longer. The gift of life and health are God's, but to assist is a God-given talent that must be used. The followers of God shall see you in a different light. Give of yourself as you will give of God, as he works through those that have His gift. You have been chosen. You must stop all other thoughts you have of not knowing your proper calling. You have been chosen, so shall you do the bidding of high.

How does a common man like me begin to accept the thought that I am capable of performing all that I have been told I must do? I cannot bring myself to accept the fact that this is something that I have done, and will do in the future. When I see what my Guides have in store for me, it scares me to think of how badly I may let them down.

July 19, 1980

SPIRIT: Have you ever been able to get whatever you wanted without first having to pay the price? Life is a bargain. You must pay for what you get. Many of life's little annoyances are no more than a charge against the good things that happened. Trust in the fact that all that is put into life shall be returned in the way we enjoy life. If little was put in, very little will be taken out of it. As the clock strikes, so does the time of judgment, for whosoever cometh and does not bring any joy onto the land, then he shall harvest no crop. As you go about life, you must never lose sight of the reason you are here, which is to complete the mystery of mankind, by giving of oneself more than one reaches for in return. The tides of time will not erase the wrongdoing; however, the test of time will. Just as Noah built the ark, so did he also fill it. Man must build his life and fill it also.

Whosoever goeth in the light of God shall perish not in the dark of hell, but shall find glory in the sight of Jesus. The light of God shines on you, go forth and do his bidding.

At this point I would like to mention that the name Rebecca was given to me while taking part in a circle. The name was to appear many times again in my writings.

July 21, 1980

Question: Sara, I have a question. Why did it take so long for Rebecca to find me?

SARA: Peter, you are not to ask this now; however, you will understand after you have met in person. We all have lived many times and are remembered for few, as eternity goes on.

Question: Will someone try to reach me in the circle we are to attend this week?

It is very possible that you will be contacted at that time. Please keep an open mind to all that happens. There are greater things in heaven than one can imagine and sometimes they are shown to others. This will be a rewarding experience for you.

Question: You, of course, will be there Sara?

Yes, where thou goeth, I shall go.

July 22, 1980

Question: Sara, will you answer questions about yourself and your past?

SARA: Yes, if you want me to.

Question: When did you last depart from the flesh?

The year of 1936.

Question: Where did you live?

I was living in Budapest.

Question: How old were you?

I was 35 years of age.

Question: Will you tell me of your past?

Yes, some of it I will tell you. Other things you must wait awhile to learn of. Just as you, I too was gifted with the ability to contact the levels beyond. I was well ahead of many others as I had the ability since childhood. As I grew older, my strength increased and I became a medium. The world was hearing of many things that were happening, but I saw them long before they actually happened. You might say that I could see the future. I have spent many lifetimes on earth; we speak now only of the last time. This is what you asked.

July 23, 1980

SARA: You are not to get involved with many outside the family about your writings, until you have become better acquainted with them. The only way you will know for sure is to have the right feeling for the people you talk with. Often it is said that no man is a fool until others call him one.

However, no man is a genius until he is discovered as well. Your gift will not be accepted by all. Some are great disbelievers, while others are ready to accept and have an understanding. It is the few who carry the load. As it was in the past, so shall it be in the future. Man is very sceptical when he does not understand that which he sees or hears. The people whom you see and feel right with will be ready to accept this, but there are those that are sceptical of God. He who follows the road shall find the inn, but he who strays too far will find nothing. The road will lead you past many hardships; as well, it will lead you to the end. Travel the road with wisdom as your guide, as he who practices his gift is sure to find the inn in many places.

July 24, 1980

Question: Sara, will great medical discoveries be made in the next few years?

SARA: Only if people are ready for it. You must have the desire to improve before medicine will help. Once the patient is of free mind and spirit it takes little extra to mend.

Question: Will cancer be cured?

There is a cure but few use it.

Question: Can you be more specific?

Yes, the facts are that many of man's remedies for cancer are a great help, but they must be used with prayer. It is only through the mercy of God that the ill shall be well again. Man may be able to improve the body for a short time;

however, without the healing of the spirit there will be no total recovery.

Question: What of the child?

The spirit has not strengthened enough to fight this battle alone. Those close must fight for him. You quest for information and you have the answers already.

July 25, 1980

SARA: When the fire is over, the world shall live in peace once again. Just as the birds fly, so shall the spirit of man.

Question: What does this mean?

That the cataclysm shall bring the fire with its destruction of many lands. After, those that are chosen will survive and will flock to God for guidance.

Question: When will this take place?

It's happening in the hearts of some now. The final breaking will come in many of your lifetimes. Man tries to conquer the space about him, and the heavens above. He travels only where spirits tend to go. Man must first set his goal and achieve fulfillment on earth before he can claim the heavens as his travel path. There is only one way to the kingdom of heaven, and it is not aboard a spaceship. Man would do well to cure the sick and the crippled before he tries flying into tomorrow. The test of time will never lose. Man shall go only as far as God sees fit to allow him. The journey through space, as you call it, is but a mere step for the spirit.

July 27, 1980

SARA: You seek an answer now?

ME: *Yes, have I known this young woman that I met at the circle before, perhaps in a past life?*

Yes, you were together in Egypt when the third Pharaoh reigned. You knew her as Rebecca, and she was your sister then. She was the younger then as now. You will meet many times more, as you will be drawn closer as time immortalizes you. She brings you love and together you shall expand your hidden powers. You shall find the first answer of many; the search for you both is over. All mankind will benefit from this reunion. Only as God's light shines on you, do you have the power of His teachings. You shall go forth and heal the threads of life that cannot mend alone. Your true test lies ahead of you, but you have found a beginning. Rebecca will remain very close to you. It is her calling to do so. Yea, the light of God will shine on you both, as the light of day shall fall on mankind. You wonder if this is all true, as you were going through many changes, but you have been waited on and now your journey is before you. Trust in God, as he will set you on your quest to seek the ill and the damned. Cure you not one, but both, as you travel through your plane. Your life is blessed with a special meaning, and you must use your gifted powers to heal once again. You have been a great healer in past lives and your powers grow as you near the final ending. The will of God is that you shall go and set your hands on he who suffers and wishes to see the light of God. For it is only he who is prepared to receive thy God that can truly be cured by the placing of the hand. Your hand is but the hand of God, extended to those that reach out for Him. All mankind is a part of God, and he who is chosen to be part of Him must choose wisely whom he lays the hand upon. Your friends have shown you a spiritual beginning. You must now begin to show them the light of God. The other young woman was drawn to you in the circle, as you had cured her before in another life. She was a leper and she came onto you and you showed the mercy of God's will and she was cleansed of all sins and went away. You have not seen her since the day of Elijah, but she has sought the power of your soul, for as she was troubled, so is she now at peace with herself. Your work has begun. You will never look back now. My time with you will be shared by others who will bring unto you many thoughts that you might share with those that follow you. Your time has come to take your place in God's glory.

*This message was signed: Your sister Sara. The reference here of sister would be in the sense that we are all brother and sister in God's eyes. I sensed a change in Sara this day.

July 28, 1980

SARA: The last meeting of the circle was a very moving spiritual experience. Many things will come of it. You will go on to practice a deeper understanding of God Almighty and will become a leader in this spiritual realm. Your time has finally come. You must now start to fit the pieces together, as they must form a pattern for your life. You are troubled that you do not know enough of the ways of the spirit world. Such is not the case. You have stored, in your subconscious mind, much wisdom of the workings of our

Lord God. It is through the mist of time that this must be drawn forward, so that you might take your rightful place as the leader of spiritual awareness. Your future holds a very great treating of soul and body. Your work is there. You must be prepared for it. Go ye not as the son of man, but go forth, as the son of God. Everlasting light shall shine on he who follows the will of God. Be ye not afraid of his calling, as no man stands alone. But when he stands in the light of Jesus, he stands in the protection of God. Go and bring a prayer and a hand of friendship unto those that need the hand of God, for as thou goest, so goest the Son of God.

July 29, 1980

SPIRIT: Peter, your travels will show you the right way. Another spirit will travel with you. Only you can control your final destiny, but many will influence you. The tasks set out are great. The calling is greater. Ask and ye shall be heard. It is your voice that will call upon the souls of eternal man to do what you have to do. Go without fear that you shall be criticized, for your gift is great and your powers will be even greater as your work begins. Worry not that you know not what to say and do; the words will be there, the deeds will be done. Verily I say unto you, sayeth the Lord, that I shall come in many ways and shall do many things before you. Trust in God and ye shall be cleansed, and the dark shall be light and the way shall be clear. Cast aside thy cane and walk with me for I am the power, sayeth the Lord, and you are my children. You shall walk with me in glory, as I have bestowed unto you the powers thy God would but have you use. Trust in the words thy God has written, in time immortal thou shalt serve me well. As my right hand doth feed me, so shall ye stand at my right hand. Worry not that the way is unclear to you, for it is I who shall show thee the way.

How can someone accept this while feeling so inadequate? This message must surely be meant for someone other than I!

July 30, 1980

SARA: The writing has changed a great deal. This is caused by your progression to higher forms of communication. The automatic writing as you refer to it, is not as high a form of communication as that which you are having now. You are progressing well and very soon you will go through yet another phase of the spiritual realm. You are about to receive all messages so that you may speak them directly as they come into your mind. This will open many doors for you, as you will be able to preach a sermon from the thoughts that enter your mind as they have been transmitted to you. The end is not in sight for you. You must accept and use this gift as you progress the rest of your mortal life. It is a great gift to be on speaking terms with the Masters; yours is such a gift. "Be not afraid of the unknown, for it is from what is unknown to us now that our knowledge of tomorrow comes." You shall live your tomorrows yesterday. The Son of God sends this gift in his Father's name. You are blessed by him. My job nears its end. Soon many more highly placed souls shall take my place. I leave you in good hands, but parting is in this case sweet, as your progress to the next plane is imminent. Few gain the height you have flown, much less to have gone on to a higher reward. The Father, Son and Holy

Ghost be with you my dear friend, as I shall journey on a trip of my own, as I too seek the true perfection of the soul. For we enter thy Father's house only with the cleansed soul and the spirit as pure as the heavens. For it is only God who has found the perfect peace and we are but to stand by his side. May love and guidance be with you always for, as you return one day, we shall meet and rejoice in thy Father's house. Go with God in your heart and the feeling of love in your soul for you have found life immortal.

**This was to be one of the last regular sessions that I was to have with Sara. It was a parting that was to touch me very deeply, as we had shared many thoughts together, some of which I do not share with you, as they were too personal. However, I was to be in contact with Sara again on a few occasions, mainly when I was under a great emotional strain. I believe that this single message holds more for me than any other I have received, as it has a sincerity that I can clearly relate to. This one message has made the entire experience worthy of a total commitment on my part; hence, the dedication of this book to Sara.*

August 2, 1980

SPIRIT: Where have you been Peter? You are feeling a loss at Sarah having gone on to another soul. The future shall hold many changes. Your daily sessions will soon become meditations of another kind. Your need for the pen will diminish like the darkened sky at daybreak. The words you speak and the thoughts that you have will be influenced by the entities here who are to help you now. The word of God must and shall reach to all mankind. Fear ye not that thy love is not strong enough to stand the test, for it has been tested many times. The word of God must be carried to all creeds and all beliefs, as together they form God's family. The door is open, you must enter here, as the next is but a step away, and someday all mankind shall step through the final door. Your concern of your strength to heal is to be put aside, for it is the strength of God that shall heal. You are but his mortal hands, and through you, shall many feel the strength of God Almighty. As he delivers yet the soul of another unto you, fear not that which ye cannot understand, for it will be made clear unto you. Your path has been chosen well, your journey is long. The tools you shall require are but a prayer to thy God, for it is unto thy God that all prayers are directed, and it is unto his children all prayers are answered. The trust of God is in all men, but for some it is clearer. For he whosoever seeketh the Lord shall find Him, and he who hideth from Him shall be found. Your journey is great, your way is clearing. You must take up the halo and fit it to the mast, for thy ship has sailed and thy sails are full. Go ye now unto thy brethren, and use the gift thy Father has sent.

August 2, 1980

SPIRIT: Peter, you are with many friends. You will learn from them the things you find meaningful at this time. Trust first in God, for it is He who shall make the final teachings. All who shall ask shall be answered. Few hear the words and few will believe. The trust that you have received, is sent as a blessing to those that will receive the final blessing. Give of yourself, as you would give to your neighbour, for it is through giving that we shall all receive our final reward. To give of oneself is to give of God, as all mankind is a true part of God. The feeling of self is but a parting of the soul; this is true, as it is spoken of in many levels of life. He who seeth the glory of God's work shall himself see the true meaning of life everlasting. One by one we shall come before our maker, and one by one we shall be accepted as his children. Only through God's hands shall the sick be well and the lame be free to walk. With the help of God, all who wish true understanding shall be at peace with themselves. As you walk, walk with a heart filled with joy, for it is thy God who has chosen you. Go now and bid him well.

August 3, 1980

SPIRIT: Only through the mercy of God shall mankind find life everlasting. Through the mercy of God's love shall come the healing of body and soul. The extended hand of the healer is but the hand of God reaching for his children in an act of comforting the spirit. As we walk with God's love, we shall walk, as he would have us, in peace with ourselves as well as with our fellow man. The act of God shall be with all who follow in his footsteps. Be not of faith for thyself, but for the sake of thy soul. May the word of God's law be followed, for he whosoever goeth with God's love in his heart, shall return unto Him in His favour. When the final meeting is upon us, we shall feel the hand on ours, lifting the burden of life from our spirit and taking our very soul unto his own. The love of God must be first, the cleansing of the soul shall follow, and the casting off of the mortal ills shall be but a following, as day follows night. The light of day shall shine brightest on he who has set his life in tune with God's law. Go ye and find the love that awaits you, for God truly loves all his children.

August 4, 1980

SPIRIT: You have taken up the challenge well. Ahead lies the damned and the inflamed. Your assistance to bring them comfort shall remain strong unto your final days. Your comfort to the soul of man will be imminent. For he who carries God's words shall himself become pure, as whosoever walketh in my footsteps, sayeth our Lord, will truly be a child of my own. For it is the love of thy Father that thou showeth, and not the will of man. Give unto Him that which you cannot give unto thyself, the feeling of peace, the words of God and the contentment to life eternal. Only as God has spoken shall his words be phrased. Only as God wishes, shall His words be repeated. Through thy teacher's gift and the encouragement of the followers, shall the word be spread unto the land. For he who cometh unto me, sayeth the Lord, shall want not, but shall find everlasting peace.

August 5, 1980

SPIRIT: You must go to the church whenever you can. They will look to you as a leader. Your teachings are to be used far and wide, for they are to help many. The path is clearing. Soon you will see the light at the end of the tunnel. There are many things that have happened, and are about to happen, that will bring you the spiritual life you are after. Your understanding of the people about you will soon be appreciated, as you will hold many more powers before the end of your mission. Take with you the thought that God has chosen you to be once again a leader of his children. As he who gains the grace of God's will, will always be held in esteem. The glory of God's words will fill a void that you have carried for many years. You knew not what was missing, but it was your love of God not being exalted by you as it had in the past incarnations. Therefore, thy house is being put in order and your life is finally turning to the will of God. For he has chosen his sons well, so that they may bring the will of their Father to the hearts of mankind. The way is clear. The path is not without holes, for it is not the way of our Lord God to set everything at ease. To labour and achieve, is but another of God's will for man. To have laboured with love in your heart is to have followed the teachings well. Your tests are tried, your goals will be many. Take up thy cross, and bear it well, for as you goeth across the land, so goeth the Lord's words. As all mankind are the children of his very being, so shall they one by one become his followers, for whosoever walketh in the path of Jesus will find life everlasting. To wander aimlessly is to shut the eyes to God. The help of many shall come to you as you prepare for your challenge. Trust in your powers, for it is through this channel that all will be found.

Walk with God.

August 6, 1980

SPIRIT: Have no fear for there is no one about to harm you. Your goal is set. Try to complete your next phase of the Spiritual realm. Your duties will be many as you take your place in the church. Slowly, you will be able to make the predictions that amaze you now. Also your powers will be used in healing the sick of body and spirit. For it is of no value to have a whole body, if the spirit lacks substance. The job ahead of you is long, the task is great; however, with the help of God, and he who works with him, you shall find a way to achieve all that is held for you. Do not tarry over little things that hold no meaning, but go on to the things God would have of you. The ways of God are many, the paths are few that will lead to glory. The way is clear for you, as many have served in your preparation. Many now come to you, or are waiting to contact you. Your friends on this side hunger to make known to you that which they are experiencing now. However, such is not the case, for as they develop, so shall their prospects for others. One must live his life in pursuit of happiness, but one must also share that happiness he finds with others.

Goodbye friend.

August 7, 1980

Question: What was my position in the church in a previous incarnation?

SPIRIT: You were a priest. The village was not too large and you were the priest of the local church. Your preaching was known far and wide as a true follower of Jesus. Few churches were able to have such a teacher as you were. Your healing was done at that time also, as your position with church and God were strong. Your life was not long however, as you died a very young man.

Question: How did I die?

You contacted a disease while trying to cure the masses. You did well, and your mercy on the sick was rewarded. When you returned this time you brought many of the healing qualities with you.

Question: When was this all happening?

In ancient Egypt.

August 8, 1980

Question: Are there many others we know who have shared a past incarnation with us?

SPIRIT: You have returned many times Peter. Your ties are many. To single them now would be to throw sand to the winds. So as ye have grown, so shall ye progress to yet another plane Your trips have been many, but your progress good. You will learn of your many trips one day, as it will be more pertinent that you understand your purpose then.

Question: Are there many people I will meet at the church that I have karmic ties with?

Yes, you will meet many over the next few years. Your teachings will come more regularly as you progress to your given position. Give it time. Your journey is long. You must rest, then carry on.

God be with you.

August 9, 1980

SPIRIT: Be of good heart, for the Lord looketh over those that hear him. Your place in God's house is waiting. The glory of God shall be seen by all mankind, for it is the last that shall return first. The work of the Spirit is unending. Your journey is near its end for the followers are about you now. Your goal in life is to bring the word of God to those that tarry over meaningless things. To have lived a life of God's bidding is to have life everlasting. There are many who will question, and will not believe in the truth. But what is truth, but only God's law. To those who do not believe, they shall be lost, but then the lost shall be found, for it is God's law that no man shall be alone. Seek and ye find the act of charity unto others is but a love of God, for it is through our charity for others that we find contentment in ourselves. Return unto him with a mind as pure as the spring rain, and your journey will be rewarded. You are not to learn and end it there, but to carry it on to others. All mankind needs a loving thought. Give of any you have, for the ear it may fall on may be troubled. God helps the followers as well as he who leads them. The past is but a darkening of tomorrow if it is not accomplished today. As you read this message, it is for all, as you have much to do. Go, with God's will at hand, and a hand extended to those that need it.

August 11, 1980

SPIRIT: With the gift to heal, comes the gift to keep mankind in a joyous mood. The gift must never be abused by anyone, for so it is given, so shall it be taken away. The Lord giveth the act of healing to make the comfort of God's will to enter unto him that needs the assistance of Christ to mend his soul. Heal the body, but also the spirit must be healed. Give unto others that which you have given your all, so that they may become as one. The spirit must be cleansed to sustain the body pure. Do not treat one without that you would cleanse all.

Question: Am I to know the identity of my Guides, now that Sara is no longer with me?

Will it help you to know she has not left from you, but she is a truly gifted part of your soul? That which she has brought to you, was through her love of God. She will never be that far away and you may call upon her if you wish. However, she is learning, as we all do, till we meet our God in perfect harmony. Yes Peter, your new guides may identify with you; however, there are many and the identity is not important. Trust in the will of God as "He only, is called by name".

This message was signed: A Friend.

August 12, 1980

SPIRIT: Well Peter, you are ready for more important things now. You no longer have to be led to gain confidence in your writings. The thought of putting some of these into print is very good, as they may help many who stand at the edge and wait. To those that can understand your way of life, they will bring much happiness when you share them. But be sure that you do just as your guides direct you. You will know what ones to use and what not to use. Your test has gone well. You are ready for a greater calling, and it is being prepared for you. Your trust in God is taken as a true love of your fellow man. However, you, as all mankind, have many things to atone for. Through your work you will pay off many of your debts, as you continue your writings and your sermons. The way is clear for you now. The stumbling blocks are put there in your way by yourself. You must find your own way over or around them. God has made your path clear, now try to walk it in the way He would have you journey to the end of the path. The way of life is not unlike that of the way of Heaven, only that you on earth must persevere to attain your goal. Eternal peace of heart and mind are hard to achieve on the earth plane, for to live attuned to God's will, will put you closer than mortals would think possible. The brotherhood of mankind is but a vehicle of God's making, to unite mankind into a whole. For it is as a whole that all return unto Him for our final reward. Put the trust of God into all that you do, and all things will take on a new light. The brighter it shines, the closer you are to God's laws. The darker it gets, the harder you must work toward perfection. ~ A friend

August 13, 1980

SPIRIT: Peter, go and find that which you must. Your search will lead you back to where you have found contentment. You must realize that very few people will share your gift. Your quest to find others may not bring you the answer you seek. Relax and let the messages flow and use them to help others. You will not be tied to the materialistic things in life forever. As you have much to do, your life must take a turn that will allow you the time to pursue the readings of God, so that you may go and spread the word as it is given to you. The changes cannot be too fast, nor can you waste valuable time. For as the sparrow flies, so does the hawk hover over, waiting to strike. The flight of his soul must be that of the dove. To have been part of someone's spiritual advancement is to be a teacher of God's law. The body is preached to today, but few take the spirit into their thoughts and prayers. It will be your blessing to receive unto your mind the thoughts and teachings of many of the true Masters of the spirit world. You must use it well. Do not attempt to set yourself aside, but continue to live as you would. The word of God reaches all mankind, but few recognize it for what it is. To be able to live and talk with the spirit is but a gift of few. Use it to help others as you go about your way in life. Soon that way will be to God's house and you shall be bid welcome. ~ A friend

August 14, 1980

SPIRIT: Peter, go unto this land and bring the word we give you so that others may find the light they seek. Open that door, for it is where thee will find the true love of God. It is there for he who seeks it. To seek and not to have found is to have left all doors closed before you. Seek and ye shall find. The love of God is found by the seekers, not by he who sits idle. The stairway to Heaven holds a new adventure in every step. This can always be a glorious experience or it can be hell in making the next step. You are the one that must take that step, therefore, it is by your actions you shall take the path of your choosing. The way to heaven is through God's front door; you must knock and the door shall be opened unto you. Go ye and bless thy Lord God, for it is through your service to him alone, that ye shall find the Kingdom of Heaven. There is much to do and so little time to prepare, lest ye return again and again. Give of yourself as you would have others give to you, for it is by giving that we shall all receive in the final ending. The Glory of God's love shines on you, as you go about His work. Be gone and return to me with yet another of thy flock. ~ A friend.

August 15, 1980

SPIRIT: Where do you go now? You must use that which has been given to you. To turn these lessons into a printed form for others would be the right thing to do. Do not wait too long, as others may find the understanding they seek from them. You will have much to publish, as you are just starting to receive that which we deem necessary for you to spread amongst the people. Many more hidden treasures will be yours when the time is right. Your mission gains more scope now, and it is time for you to begin taking a lead yourself. There are many things to learn, and such little time to learn it in. You must not just wait idly by. Prepare your writings soon, and be prepared to journey into yet another deeper understanding of man. For when you are chosen to receive, so shall ye return unto others, for it is all God's children that must some day be pure of heart and soul again. The trust of God, and he who helps you, shall see you through the roughest of times ahead. For the strong shall lead the weak and gather in the fields, and marvel at that which is the glory of God's work. For is it not beholding of Angels to see the flowers bloom, and the birds fly. All that is created of God is but a part of God. Man and the universe are also but a part of God's making. For He would have that we enjoy all, as we will someday rejoin Him and the Heavens will be filled with joyous singing. Weary that ye may be, always set aside a moment for God to enter unto you and let His glory be the light that guides you. ~A friend

August 16, 1980

SPIRIT: We are but an instrument of God. As we go about our daily work we forget that we have a strength to call on to help us lift the burden of life from our shoulders. When the going is great, the Spirit of God is there to enter unto us, and give of Himself to us. So shall we give unto others, for is it not so that "so shall the willow bend, as the winds blow." The facts of life hereafter, are like the blowing wind; they shape the soul as it awaits the final journey. Try not to imagine that which the human mind cannot conjure, for the hereafter is a place of beauty that no man can imagine. The teachings of streets of gold are but fairytales; the need is not there. For it is a life of the spirit to journey to the far reaches of the Universe at the twinkle of the eye. To recognize your neighbour you will recognize his soul as it is at peace with God's love. The pressure of life on your plane is but an oxen pulling a loaded cart. When the work is done, then shall ye rest in the peace and loving care of God, for to have sinned against thy God is to have lived the normal human life. All is not lost through the sins of man, but he must atone before he journeys to the highest plane. It is there he must be at peace with his Maker, for it is the final resting place. ~ A friend

August 16, 1980

SPIRIT: Yes, there are many answers to your questions. To think them through you will need an eternity of man's lifetimes. As we progress we will find answers for many things we do not now question. The light is strongest where the darkness falls. Try to think of life as a journey to a pleasant ending. Just to live is but a wonder of the Universe. Life is sent through God and it is taken away by God. Not as a price for sin but to gather unto Him all that He loves dearly. To enter unto the field with God as the shepherd, is to be in a flock that is protected forever. We are but lambs in the flock of life. Giving of ourselves to God's glory will bring a happiness that man can never experience here. The true test of God's love is His receiving of all His children unto Him as life eternal. The light is there - follow it till the brightness is but a glow upon you, for to gather unto Him your life is to complete the journey set for mankind. Open the door to a new life each day as you progress to a greater understanding, and all things that are worthy of God's love shall come about. Will the love of God shine as you enter His house?

August 18, 1980

While sitting in a circle with a few friends, one very spiritual member commented that she had a vision of an old Indian spirit by my side. When told of this I felt compelled to ask my spirit guides about it. This is the answer I received.

SPIRIT: Yes, it is the spirit of Running Deer. He has been watching you for some time now. He will be a spirit of great strength to you. He is one of many, but he does make himself present about you always. I have a message for you now:

Try to get closer to God, for it is through the love of God that man shall attain the heights of Heaven. Your progress is good, your heart has been opened, and the word of God is now in you. Do not be alarmed if you are to go through many changes, for it is all destined to be for you. As you go, you will have a host of angels that shall protect you. You have not yet received the full impact of this change to you, but when it comes, you should be ready for it. The words of God are used in many ways, not all are wrong, and not all are right. The feeling that is received, while we are in harmony with God's will, is the most glorious feeling, that it cannot be overlooked. Give unto others that which is received unto you, as all mankind are not as fortunate to be able to listen. ~ A friend

August 19, 1980

SPIRIT: Only by God's command, shall ye bring unto others that which is brought unto you. The words of God are for mankind to find the peace that brings true love. May the guides of old be at your side as you call upon thy Father's help, for it is as a true believer lives, that someday all men will live again. To be in harmony with God's law, is to be as light as a cloud and as bright as a star, for it is man who holds back mankind. It is through his deeds and misdeeds that man's progress is ever so slow. The true test of God's law is to live as he would have you live. To attain the pinnacle of success in your life is but to take the first step on the stairway to the Heavenly House. The stairs are straight, but man puts many bends in them as he tries to attain the ultimate goal. If man would but stop and listen to his heart as well as his head, he would hear the message that is there for him. It is not about getting to the top of the steps, but how you attain the next step that counts. To have attained the top is to take your place in oneness with the Lord God. As one, the universal love will hold you forever extended in eternal peace. For a goal such as this, is it not worthy of mankind's efforts to better himself in preparation for that glorious beginning? The power of God's love shall be the only way to enter unto the Kingdom of Heaven, for it is there that mankind comes closest to God. ~A friend

August 20, 1980

SPIRIT: The doorway to a new future comes from the proper use of meditation. You will find the answers to many of the things that puzzle you from the inner soul. The one thing you must remember is to ask for guidance, so that your own guides will be there to help you. Pray for protection so that nothing will scar your soul. The time for meditation is when you have time to be alone, and very quiet, as you must concentrate on being one with God. It takes time, so do not hurry into it, as you will not get the desired results. Peter, you must try to set aside time for researching your readings, and making them ready to publish. This must be done soon. Your time is full, but you must put aside less important things. God's will is that no man will go without hearing of His word. To be part of this carrying of the word is but a blessing from God. Your Akashic record will show of your deed, and you shall be rewarded in Heaven. For whosoever goeth the way of our Lord God shall find peace eternal. There are so many things left to do that you must go about them as often as you can. Man is in need of guidance and few will take time to help him. Your flight through this lifetime will be marked as a messenger; now go and carry the word. ~ A friend

August 21, 1980

Question: Do I have other entities with me, other than the old Indian?

SPIRIT: Yes, they are amongst many that look over your shoulder. The Indian man gives you the strength to carry on your daily tasks. He asks little in return, except that you do rest when you need it. His spirit is very strong, and his fearlessness has helped you face many problems.

The elderly man from Egypt is a new follower to you. He will bring you comfort in the writings of our Lord. He will help you when you set to putting this all to print. His knowledge is vast, and he wishes you to absorb as much as possible of it through these writings. You may call on his wisdom whenever you need help. He is there to assist you.

The young woman is learning from your experience. She learns with you, but she also will bring you the feeling of God's love as she watches over you.

These entities will change from time to time; however, they will always come back to see how you are doing. Your attachment to some will be stronger than others. Walk in haste, as you have much to do. ~ A friend

August 22, 1980

SPIRIT: Will you give unto God your very soul? For it is through giving that all things shall be received. To give of one's true heart is to give all, for the breath of life is but nothing. To reach a oneness with God is all and life immortal; it is God's goal for all of us. Some will take an eternity of time to achieve this goal, but the spirit will continuously strive for this perfection. Let no man think he is worthy of God's love. Only by living a life, or lives, of virtue can one ever hope to attain this. However, God is love, and love is forgiveness, and God is a forgiving God. He will cast upon the wind the sin of mankind so that his spirit will dwell with Him forever. Man is but a mobile in a wind tunnel; the more he moves the further he gets from his goal, but to cease the wind he will stand in peace, ready to meditate that which is his goal. The love of God will touch all, but many do not feel that first touch and will turn away ever to have to return again and again. The love of mankind was given as a gift of life. To journey down through life and not try to attain a feeling of true love is a lifetime wasted. For is it not written that to enter God's house we must truly love thy God? Only through our deeds do we show this love, and only through our misdeeds do we neglect this love. The light shall shine on he who has found His secret, for love is eternal. ~ A friend

August 23, 1980

SPIRIT: You are to give unto all that which you receive, for it is through giving that the glory of God's love shall be felt throughout the land. Go ye and spread your written word.

As the crow flies, so shall man's spirit be lifted by the words ye write. Give not into the temptation of the weak, and sit idly by, but go forth and bring this work to those who await it, for in all mankind there lies a spark waiting to be kindled into flame. A word spoken or written is all that it takes to move them to greater heights. The gift of outer communication is given but to few, and you are a chosen one. Go and do the bidding of your Masters, for it will set well with all when you have made your round. Go not to the poor alone, but go to the rich and famous, for all people have a yearning for truth. The final truth is but the ability to look unto thy God and say, "I have returned to be but again in oneness with my Master". The Lord God goes with you my friend, and may your journey be long. But, however long it is, use that which ye have received for all. ~ A friend

August 25, 1980

SPIRIT: Only you can tell when your debts are paid, but you never are the one to keep score. As the child grows older it makes mistakes; as the adult grows older it makes many, many mistakes. But as the spirit grows closer to God, He alone will score. He alone will give the forgiveness to become pure of heart, to dwell in His house. Give unto them that need it the help to guide their ways, but the claiming of the soul is but the work of God. For whosoever worketh in the name of God, shall first have found mercy in God's love. The work of our Lord is carried by many, but the saving of the soul is only unto God. Let not that ye shall wander unto this land like the sheep separated from its flock, but find ye new horizons. Keep the temple of God's love in sight always. Man is never lost if he has the light of God shining about him, for he is on the road to the Kingdom of Heaven. At the end of his journey, he will find yet his father and his mother and theirs and theirs. For it is on the resting place of souls that we contemplate that which we have accomplished and we will know that which we did not. To begin life again, we must be born again. Life is a round of mistakes and learning, for how else will ye return unto God but as a spirit pure as He would have you. Live as you will, but learn in the process that God can be reached in only one way.

August 26, 1980

May I ask a question please?

Yes, any time.

What door will open next for me?

SPIRIT: The door to happiness is always open. It is there for anyone to journey through. Your life shall become that of the sage, for you shall be given the power to see. Only through the love of God will man be at peace. While there are wars and strife about the world, no man shall know total peace on earth. When the leaders of the nations find the love of God in their hearts to fill the wanton lack of faith they now hold, then the world shall see a living peace. It will be many times thy children's children that this will come to be, as we do not have highly evolved souls in great numbers with us now to control these things. In years, nay in centuries to come, man will have progressed to a higher way of life. His soul will be redeemed of many of his present ways. The world will not stop for the lack of faith of so many, for so few. Nay it is through the growth of the spirit that the returning will bring peace. Man has but one fault, that of doubt. He cannot see that God has put before him an altar. He has but to go before that altar and pray. The glory of God shall pass no man, for it is through his mistakes that he returns to cleanse the soul and prepare for life everlasting. Go, for the door opens.

August 27, 1980

SPIRIT: You are to go about your life as you normally would. Many things can and will happen that will alter this life. Your present employment may change. You may also change your social life as well. The door to the future is open. You must decide whether to step through or not. Only through prayer shall you see the light, and when you do, you will know which fork to take. The ways of our God are many and his ways unto you are many. Keep the work of God, for it is through this work that all else will seem trivial. Trust in the Spirit Guides, as results will be alarming to you, as the knowledge that they will bring to you will be great. It is not that you only have been chosen, but that you also have chosen your way. The inner soul shall have precedence over man, and where it is contested by the personality there can be great conflict. In your case, the inner soul has found harmony with the personality. Go forth about your life, but know well that you no longer travel alone. Your Guides are there to help you always. Their devotion to you is in part their devotion to mankind. For as a Godly Soul on your side progresses, they too progress to a higher understanding of the creation of man. The learning process goes on and on, until the final lesson, that of pure love.

God be with you.

August 28, 1980

SPIRIT: You were chosen because you have a sincere desire to help your fellow man. It is not for someone else to judge God, but for God to judge us. You, my friend, have so been judged. Do not let it worry you that you will not know what comes next; all things will happen in the proper time. The way is open for another sage to bring a message; you may well be able to clear the way. All mankind at some time question their positions; at times it is only common to. But do not forget, as we progress each time we return, we are getting a greater understanding of God's law. Why do you think that there seems to be so many different denominations of churches? It is through these different teachings that God's way will be made known to all mankind. The teachings may vary, but the meaning should remain the same. Man is looking for his beginning and his creator. The true meaning of life can fill many books for some; for others it can be summed up in but a sentence. The true love of God is not felt until we return unto him, as a pure soul, so we return to the flesh in many ways so as to go about the learning process. All journeys must end and the supreme journey shall end at God's door. And when ye do He shall say, "Enter into the Kingdom of God my child, as you have proven yourself well." for no man enters unto His door, unless he is prepared. Then all things shall be as one, and one thing shall be as all.

As Told To Me

August 29, 1980

SPIRIT: Let the earth and sky signal the closing of another race. For with the coming of each new generation there are the ones who leave the planet Earth. As life evolves, so does the soul of man, for it is through birth, death and rebirth that mankind move on to another plateau. For some it will be an eternity of coming and going, yet for others we tarry here but for a while. The progress of man's development is beyond comprehension, if he was but to accept the fact that life can be controlled by the inner spirit of man. For it is in the inner spirit that the true man dwells; the outer shell we carry about is but a state of suspension made to create a burden for the soul. Only through the perfection of life can you perfect the spirit to attain the true meaning of life. The willow will bend in the wind, but the gentle breeze will also move it in beauty as it sways to the rhythm of nature. Man must also learn to bend with the hardships that befall him, but also learn to be in harmony with nature. The true meaning of life is but a mirror of our past. As life evolves so is death inevitable, for it is nature's true cycle of being. We live, we die, but in between we must serve the purpose of our being - that of praising God for the glory of life. Without life, the soul would not perfect itself to oneness with God. All men are equal for God, as the creator, made you so. It is through perfection that some become leaders of others.

August 30, 1980

SPIRIT: You are about to find an answer to one of your questions. To live and not have performed one of the duties of mankind is to have lived without total meaning. Man's act must first be to man, then to God. For was it not God's law that said, "Do unto others as you would do unto me." It is through the act of doing unto others that the soul finds contentment that it requires to perfect its true self. Man must learn to seek that which is better for his fellow man, before he can find the benefits of life's pleasures for himself. It is through giving of God's greatest gift, that of love, that will bring true happiness. For unto him that giveth his love, so shall he receive the Kingdom of Heaven as he has followed in his Father's steps. Only they, who give the gift of love, give the true and only lasting gift. As I give to you, so shall ye give to your brother, and only when it is lost shall the grieving be felt. You are about to be tried once more, as you are about to face yet another of life's tasks. Share your thoughts with others, so you may receive that which you seek. The road to eternity has many windings; however, he who sees in the dark shall not fear the light of day. Your load increases, but so shall ye receive the guidance ye seek. The Lord shall look over thy shoulder as ye go on your way.

August 30, 1980

SPIRIT: The sounds of nature are but the singing of God's spirit. The acts of nature are but the glory of God's love. To hear and not to be in tune is to be searching for that which ye shall not find. The act of nature unto man is but to live a life of judgment that will cleanse the soul of man. You cannot look into a bush and see a rose, if a rose cannot grow in it. So is life. Many will flower to beauty and perfection, some will wither and the thorn shall be that of the flowers. The way is clear that to harvest the flower you must clean the field of weeds. The end of each day will bring the beginning of tomorrow, but tomorrow is but an extension of today. You must know that you have perfected each seed today, so that the harvest will be pure tomorrow. Through time, man has gained strength in the beauty of the flowers he gathers, but he cannot always gather without feeling the thorn.

Right after having received the above message, a small circle of friends began a discussion as to when life begins. The following is the result of this discussion, after asking my guides for their participation.

Question: At what time does the spirit enter the body?

At the time of conception the decision is made, but only at the first breath does the soul enter into life. The body is pure, but it is not whole until the spirit has completed entry. The child's first cry is the sound of the spirit. From there on, it remembers nothing of its previous life; all things are in a state of suspension. This is the quiet time and resting time for the spirit. As the child grows, so awakens the spirit. Do not give unto yourself that which you cannot hold. Go about your learning in a way you will hold that which is sent to you. The meaning of life is life itself. So few can see the beauty of life. As we age, we see change, but do we see the perfection of the soul? He who can see his perfection is ready to return.

September 3, 1980

MARTHA: Open your hearts O men of Israel, as you are not on the path to God. The current state of affairs in the earth today is manifested in the lack of love of God. Man thinks too much of his borders and his landholdings to take time to share a love with God. He does not use the laws of God to live by, but takes carnal sin as his host. Man must return to the land and the sea, and look for God. It is only through the light of day that man's eyes see. When he learns to walk in darkness unafraid, he will once again find his way back to a life with God. The King of Kings returns to show the way; follow and ye shall see the doorways to the heavens unfold. It is through these doors all must pass. Jesus said unto man "Go ye and find the love of God, and ye will find the love of all things." The words you write are words of hope for many. Do not cherish and hold them back but give them unto others less fortunate so they too may hear the word of God. Your book begins to leave a message of the Word for man. You must work on it. It will continue to be a great help to you, but also will help others. As you go, go in the trust that God has for you. You shall journey in the peace that only God can control.

This was the first of what would be many messages from Martha. Martha would go on to lift the content of each message to yet greater heights. She was indeed a gifted Spirit Guide.

September 4, 1980

Question: Can you tell me the origin of cancer and what the cause for it is and the cure?

SPIRIT: First, it is a plague mankind has brought onto himself. The nervous system is the start of it. From there, the body is out of harmony with many things. Only as the body functions naturally will you ward off cancer. The cure is known to man but seldom used. You must use the beet top and a natural honey with a few almonds. Make a tea from this and drink at least three times a day. But along with this you must cure the spiritual body as well, as nothing will put the body back in harmony if the spirit has not also been cared for. The healing for cancer should always include meditation so that the body gets time when all stress is removed. Only God will have the final say, so it is important that prayer be used always. Man will continue to try to procure a serum for this, but it is not something that will work without the work of God. There are many who seem to be cured, and then relapse into yet another deeper stage of this plague. To comfort the body and not the soul, is to comfort but a part of you. Unless all is comforted, the body is out of harmony with the universe about us, and the spirit shall return. It is God's law that man be kept in harmony with Him, as he set up our very being to return to Him pure. Time is the factor that must be overcome. Some people use it well, while others are used well by time.

September 5, 1980

MARTHA: Never think of Heaven without first thinking of God. For as one is all, so all is one. The act of God has created in man's mind the power of seeing more than he can understand. You must use the power given to you to better use. God created all men equal, but many end up the servant of others. It is through this servitude of God, that we shall progress to a better soul. While we waste time on the less important side of life, the true meaning slips past us and we wonder what life is all about. To watch the eagles soar is to have the wings of Angels, for it is at the lofty heights that the eagle can find that which it searches for. So it is for man. If he could but attain the loftier heights, he would truly see tomorrow. It is through man's sight that he trusts much of his belief, for if he does not see it happen, he has doubts. God gave man a mind of his own to think about those things which he does not understand, and to learn about them. Too much time is spent on the material things in life instead of spending time contemplating what is real. Life is a mystery to man, and it will remain so, for it is not meant that man shall ask or seek and find his answer to everything. Life is sacred. It was given by God and it shall return unto God. While you have it, use it well and protect it from that which man has put in its way. The true meaning of life is felt only when we leave this flesh body and return to the spirit whole, for it is God who sent us and God who calls us back.

September 6, 1980

SPIRIT: Open your heart, for the love of God enters only where He is welcome. As you walk the road, try to walk with God for no man shall be lost, if he walks with a companion. As you leave the life you live and journey to the other side, you will find things of beauty unbelievable to the human eye. For here, all things are as they are meant to be; nothing has been changed by man. The sights are unlike anything that can be described on earth. The colors are so radiant, and yet so soft. The flowers are so delicate, yet strong and with fragrance so pure. The sky is a blue you have never seen and the clouds are like huge balls of fluffy powder. As you walk, you do not take the halting steps of man, but glide effortlessly over the path of your choosing. So glorious is the setting sun, that all will stop to watch that which God has created. When you feel rest is needed, it is but to stop and meditate. Your feelings and all things will become quiet, as if the earth has stopped. To communicate with the many that have come before you, is but a joy to behold, for they are waiting to lead you beyond the gates of Heaven. For Heaven is not the final place, but a resting place, so as to gain the spiritual strength to journey about God's domain. Prepare as you can, for the change is great. All mankind shall go this way, but for some it is easier to adjust to it. Keep the love in your heart and kindness in your thoughts, as all will come together here.

September 6, 1980

Question: What can you tell me of the 12 apostles?

SPIRIT: Only God's law said there were 12. The facts are there were 13. The apostles were there to follow and learn the true meaning of God's words, and bring the meaning unto man. The apostles are as real as God's love of man. Only through the love of God do we find the true understanding of life. Through the apostles this meaning was carried to all mankind.

Go unto the hill, for it is there that you will be closer to God.

You have not had a complete answer to your question, as the answer is not to be had at this time. Many men think they know the answer to all things in Heaven and earth, but they are lost in the mind of man. The true answers are not in books, but in the heart. Heed the inner spirit, for it too has the answer you seek. All things have a meaning, but there are many meanings for all things. Seek the truth in your soul for it can answer many things. To try to outthink one's spirit is but to talk against the wind. Truth is love and love is truth.

September 8, 1980

MARTHA: Would ye not go unto the hills, for there the lost shall be found. Jesus found the stranded lamb and said unto the shepherd, "Protect thy flock, for unknown dangers lie waiting." The people have listened to his words preached from many pulpits, but the meanings vary as to the light of day. Repeat only that which is given, for what has been written by man is not all God's words, for seek ye not the answers upon the hill, when the questions lie in the valley. Man was created in the sight of God to manifest himself to live with nature, not to have to atone for his act against nature. Do not give of oneself only of the love of God, but give of the love of mankind, as is this not also a part of God. The things that happen around us are but a signal that all things live and breath through the gift of life made manifest by God. To live a life of disharmony is to journey and find the inn closed, and find not the contentment of the safety within. Man makes many trips he cannot complete, but he must bear in mind he has to face the return to the final ending unless his spirit is to dwell in constant turmoil within. As the light of day brightens the hours after darkness, so should the spirit be lightened unto Him, and return ready to serve only that which is a part of Him. God's mercy will let the spirit return many times to gain that perfection, and it is through the experience of life that life everlasting is attained. The glory and love of God is for all mankind; you have but to accept it. Man is but a projectile in space, hurling unto his final resting place, at one with God.

September 9, 1980

MARTHA: Lo the world awaits the coming of Christ, but Christ is in all mankind. Go not unto your Father's house only to say a prayer, as God will hear them from anywhere. The glory of God shines on high. All mankind will follow the same path, but for some the way is easier. The start of each new day is a day closer to the return of the spirit. For, as much as it beckons unto man's call, so shall it return first to its Father, Our Father, whom art in heaven. The trust we put into ourselves is but a passing of what God has put unto mankind. For it was through his only begotten son Jesus, that the sins of man have been redeemed. But, we must still atone for our misdeeds unto our fellow man, for it is God's law and the law of the Universe, that all men were created equal and shall return unto God as pure souls. The test of time, and of many lifetimes on earth, are the price we pay for our return unto Him. The art of prayer is but a thank you to our Father God for all things given unto us. For man alone can never open Heaven's door; it must be opened for him. You have not completed the cycle of life until the spirit is resting in peace, on the next side of Heaven. He who takes life as a gift, shall find his reward, but for those who treat life as something lower than God meant it to be, shall find the way hard. Only the followers of God's law shall find the true meaning of Heaven, for they dwell there now. Only the ones that tarry, and waste that which has been given, shall find the light hard to find, for they live in eternal darkness. God is pure, and so shall mankind be when he returns to Him.

September 11, 1980

MARTHA: Will you do anything for your brother? This is a question that everyone should ask themselves. Unless you can do something for someone else, you cannot do for yourself, as that which ye do unto others will surely be done unto you. For so sayeth the Lord God almighty. As we go about our daily work we forget these things, and do not always do as we should. To try to live a greater meaningful life, we must be prepared to accept that which does not always suit us. The problems of today's world are at part the greed for oneself, for it is the common thing to look after oneself before thinking of thy brother. The pressures of modern living are great against the spirit, for it truly knows what should be done. However, the carnal spirit is more apt to be heard. The glory of God's kindness is there for the asking, but you must do unto others the kind deeds to receive it. Go into the night, and give not into fear, for the light of God within you shall show you the way. For he who is lost is lost only unto himself, for God knows thy presence. Travel with God and the soul shall never be lost. Only unto man did God entrust the mind to think on such a level. The birds and beast and the serpent can but do their bidding, but cannot think such as man. Mankind must not become attached too greatly to the earthly body, as it is a temporary mode of travel, and a chance to pay karmic dues. Oneness with God will come when all dues are paid and the spirit is ready to dwell with God on high.

September 12, 1980

MARTHA: The acts of God are not all known to man. Few mortals can imagine what it is like on this side. There are many things to do here. You can rest when you first enter, but then you must start your work with others. The manual tasks you are used to are not necessary, but there are other things that must be done. Many souls pass over that are not ready to come, as some are frightened by the thought of accepting physical death. Some do not realize that the spiritual life remains forever. Many want to go back, but it's impossible if life has left the mortal body. A few come just before death and take a look and choose to stay, others to return. If the spirit is kept active, the way yours is, you will truly know the meaning of what is happening to you when you cross over. But for those who have no conception of the spiritual life hereafter, they will find it much harder, so many spirits here work with the new arrivals and try to bring the spiritual message to them. It is very hard to control a spirit whose life has been taken by another, or by accident while on your side. The thought of it being a bad dream that will go away and they will return to their loved ones on earth is always strong. But for those who know the final step has been taken, the glory of God awaits them, for none shall miss the love of God, for He is love and He is God. We all return to God, as we are a part of Him. Trust in your spirit and let it grow, for it shall be thy salvation.

September 15, 1980

MARTHA: The day of reckoning, as you call it, is yet a ways away. To forget that we, as God's children, have a role to play in everything that happens will leave very little doubt as to the necessity of another world calamity. The end of the world, as is referred to, is not something that is imminent. It can be altered, as God can alter that which He deems unnecessary. Only he who follows the ways of God will be ready to accept the changes. Only he who holds God's law and love as eternal shall cross over without the dread of death as he journeys to this side. The acts of man will never be as that of nature. As the wind blows, and the lightning falls, man is held in awe of the power of nature. Only as nature reacts to man does he fear it, for it also brings the beauty and fulfillment that man needs to live on the planet earth. You are not going to see the total devastation of earth, but a great shifting of it. The end is not inevitable, but only man's lifetime on earth is inevitable, for he shall live and die and when he dies, he returns to the spirit once again.

September 16, 1980

The following is the writing I received while with a group of friends. We were discussing the crystal skull that had been the subject of a newspaper article. I am including this writing as some may find it interesting.

Question: Can you tell me anything about the Crystal Skull?

SPIRIT: Yes I can. It was made many centuries ago by followers of the Buddhist faith. The skull is an unknown substance to mankind, as it is formed of an unknown substance of earth. The substance came from another galaxy and was formed by the Tibetan monks who use the power of mind over matter. This enabled them to shape it to the perfect shape it has taken. The skull holds many powers, but all contact with these powers was lost many thousands of years ago. Today it sits on display for all to see, or all are on display for it to see. The skull has the capacity to think and answer when you take a problem to it. It also can fulfill some of these prophecies. The skull was made to contain the thoughts and wisdom of man, and this is what it has done. No thought form comes before it that it does not store. Its gift of wisdom is great. Man should be trying to unlock the hidden door to within, as centuries can unfold unto him who finds the key. The facts of life are there as well as the history of your planet. For as it happened, so has the skull recorded it. Go, if you can and view this skull as it will not always remain in your country. It truly belongs to mankind, but it has never been studied as a link to the past, for it is looked upon as a piece of spiritual trappings that holds no meaning other than the artwork of creation. Truly it holds answers to creation itself, if only the link could be found to its wealth of information. Only God can lead you to the secrets within; try not to second-guess it, as it is beyond mankind.

September 17, 1980

MARTHA: Tarry not, for all is in God's hands. He who shall stand by the word of God shall stand by His side. You are not going to be able to journey forth unto the land when you are harnessed to reality. Only to he who wishes the change, shall it happen. He who goes forth over the mountain shall have the view from the top. But for he who stays in the valleys, the sites shall never be beholding unto him. As you go over, you reach the pinnacle, and you have reached a nearness with God and his creation. The paths are many, and few, if any, find the right one the first time. Journey forth and seek the path, for it is there for all to see. The glory of God shall shine on he who follows the path to everlasting life. For, it is God's path, and it leads unto Him. Many are lost and many cannot see, but for a prayer, the way shall be shown unto you. Go unto the hills, for there the pathway widens, and it is easy to follow once you have found the way. The stairway to Heaven is very steep for some; for others it is but a short walk. Man has brought upon himself many weights that he must carry. Until he can cast them off, his way will be greatly burdened. But the greater sins were cast off by the love of Jesus, for was he not crucified for his love of man. Your burdens are man-made and can be cast aside any time, for they hold not thy spirit, but only thy flesh. The word of God says that God is thy Master, but to some thy burden becomes thy master and there is little or no time for God. Think you well as you take upon you new burdens, for all must have time to pray with thy God, for He is the Almighty.

As Told To Me

September 18, 1980

MARTHA: There are many kinds of wisdom. Some make you a stronger spiritual person; others make you a stronger physical person. The wisdom you seek is for the spirit, as you show this in your thoughts. The light of day should brighten many things for man; however, many are still left in darkness. To see the true light man must give of his soul to God. He must show a desire to live that which he seeks. He must always show a love of God and his fellow man, as to complete the cycle of earthly existence. Wisdom is gained through many channels, the least of which is study. You must live your life according to God's holy law, for it is the only way to total wisdom. The shepherd sits and awaits his flock as they graze on the hill and meadow, but he does not sleep nor waste his time on frivolous thoughts. The shepherd studies the heavens for stars, and marvels at nature and learns from what he sees. Only if time is left to idly slip by does one miss the opportunity to learn more about the world he lives in. All acts of nature should be studied, as they are an important link with the final ending. The act of love by the father for his family, is a lesson in wisdom, for is it not comforting to the soul? Many things are said to be beyond man's reach, but few things really are, for he who reaches for the highest fruit will receive the sweetest taste. As in life, one must continue to reach higher than before if he is to learn of new tastes. He, who reaches for the highest, reaches for God, and He will take thy hand.

September 19, 1980

SPIRIT: Thou art thy staff. Live by this law and the way will be clear for thee. One must set the God within him upon the altar. Cleanse thy soul by doing unto others that which is manifest in the God within. Do all things as you would do unto thy Father God, for only until then shall thy staff support thee. God gave unto man the power to think and do many things. In return, man was to live with love in his heart for all who share the world about him. The love one feels for others is thy God, self expressing His love for all. As we grow in God's love, so shall we give of God's love to others, for whosoever cometh unto Me without love in his heart shall return unto flesh again and again. The power of God's love is likened to the heavens above, for He loves all things in His creation. But man is above all beast and crawling things and must be held in a higher understanding of life, for he can return to his maker a better soul, if he but tries. Only as one of God's children do we visit on the plane of flesh. We learn of the good and the unpleasant things of life as they exist, but the temptations have been manifested in the mind of man. God put man here as a temple of the spirit, to dwell in happiness and love for one another. Through man's lack of foresight, he has lost much of his spiritual following, for he has taken unto himself the gift of life and abused it. Only through the worshiping of thy God shall the true meaning of life exist, for to worship man or that which man has made manifest is to worship a false God .

September 21, 1980

SPIRIT: Thou goeth the way of Jesus, for before him came the harbinger. God's love of his children is the purest love of all. Be not afraid when the crossing cometh, for many will be there to greet thee. The Lord sayeth unto His people that all things shall be as it has been. The God of all mankind shall reign supreme. Lo, the traveler that strays in the night shall find his way, if he asks for the way to be shown unto him. Walk without fear, as fear is but a figment of the mind's manifestation. Fear itself cannot harm thee unless you bow to a creation, and not to God. Man must find his soul, and make it known to his creator, that there is but one God. The lifetime of man is spent in searching for oneself, for loved ones, and for his creator. Unless the search is complete man will not be ready to accept death from the flesh body, for it is only a temporary housing of the soul. When death comes, as it must, all feelings of earthly things must leave and a return to the spirit shall be all consuming. Death is but another door that shall be opened when you knock, for did not thy God say to you "Knock and it shall be opened."

September 22, 1980

The following is another question that was asked while at a group meeting.

Question: Is there something in the Devil's Triangle that does consume ships and planes?

MARTHA: Yes, it is the Giant Crystal of Atlantis. It is still active, and will remain so, as time will never destroy the strength of the crystal. It is still giving out its power, as it was never discharged when it slid into the sea. It shall remain a truly great power forever. Man may someday find this treasure, but if he does, it will only destroy him again. The power the crystal holds is more power than man should possess, as the destructive power is awesome. Man has produced his own weapons of power now, but they will never rival the power of the Giant Crystal. No man should ever have this power again.

September 23, 1980

SPIRIT: When will the end come for all who do not believe in the Lord God Almighty, and will not do His bidding? For they have reached the end, when they forsake thy God. No man can live a life of contentment with himself, and with other men, if he has but lost his faith in the Almighty. If man has the power to see, he should be able to realize that there is a greater force behind the life that we share, than the act of breathing. To hold on to life as it was given, is to praise God for all that we have, and shall be given. The act of love unto His children is the total commitment of love. The child shall love in return. God so loved the world and all things on it that He gave his only begotten son, so as to cleanse the earth of all that was not holy. Only as the laws of the land are obeyed, shall all mankind live in the peace that was meant to be. Many lives are lost as man continues to war against mankind. All wars are an act against God, for He made the Heavens and Earth to hold out to man the place he would dwell in true love. Man has placed himself above the power of God. He shall feel the repentance that must be. God created man to manifest as unto Him, and live in harmony with all God's creation.

September 24, 1980

MARTHA: Only as you go about your battle, will you know thy foe. Give of thy service to God, as he alone can give unto you eternal bliss. The love of God shall shine upon he who works with God, for he shall tend the flocks. Only as you see the work of God, shall ye find the true spirit of Christ. Through many centuries man has begun to put self and tangibles before God in his house. The true meaning of God's love can be felt only when mankind is prepared to put God before all worldly things, above all, to put God before self. For is it not God who sits on high? Man shall toil at many things, his life filled with aches and sorrows, but if he holds a place in his heart for the love of God, he shall overcome his sorrow. For is it not karma? Mankind has yet to overcome many obstacles if he is to live the life that is allotted to him. The peace and joy that could be attained on earth would be something to behold, if man were to return to being a Godly creature. As it was in the beginning, so shall it be again, for God so loves us all, that he shall someday repent all sins once again on earth, and all will live in God's love and will honour thy God once more. Man must learn to live with himself and his neighbour before he can ever live with God. Many things shall change; however, the way of the heart must be changed by man, for he too must be prepared for this.

September 25, 1980

INFINITY: Death is a beautiful thing if it is looked upon as a step closer to thy God on high. For it is through death that the spirit returns, and the soul becomes pure. As you grow older the thought of death can be accepted more than it can at an earlier age, as the spirit begins to long for the return to this plane. But living is the only way to pay for our wrongdoings, and karma is karma. Life is and can be most beautiful as we go about our lifetime on earth, doing that which will comply with God's law. The Son of God became man, so as to show the way, and all mankind have His path to follow. God be with you my friend. ∞

This was the first message signed with the symbol for INFINITY.

September 26, 1980

SPIRIT: Give unto him that goes before you, as he has lightened thy path. As the darkness turns to light, the way that has been taken is truly clear unto thee. All roads have a fork, but all do not lead to Heaven. Indeed no road leads to Heaven without that thou hast done thy bidding well. For Heaven shall be experienced upon thy earthly plane, and hell also, shall be known to many. Mankind is constantly faced with decisions he must address and they are not always easy. The one chosen is not always right, but to fail is but to be human. For is living not a learning experience from beginning to end? How many days go by that one does not hear of something new, or makes a mistake in something that they do? Only in the spirit body shall ye possess the qualities ye seek in the flesh body. They are there all the time but many are governed by the flesh only. To explore thy inner being is to explore the universal living organisms, for all things were created from God, by God, and shall return unto God. Mankind struggles to learn, but thy knowledge is in thee. Look and ye shall find.

September 27, 1980

SPIRIT: You may take awhile to clear your mind, but you may never clear the subconscious mind. All thoughts and deeds are recorded there; as the clock strikes the hour, many more deeds are done. Only to have lived the life of a holy man can you be without sin of deed. Be of good faith and thy thoughts shall follow in the pattern as all things have their place. Love is but a word until it is felt between man and woman, but the joy it brings to feel the love of God is but comparable to no other. Only as a child of God do we learn the true meaning of life. Life is not just a span of time in the mortal state, but is eternal. Immortality is truly a thing that can be looked upon as part of our soul. To live many lifetimes as many different people, is but to allow thy soul to flourish and to learn, and above all, to reach the pinnacle of learning, to be in oneness with thy Creator. Life serves more purpose than to populate the earth, for it is through life that we grow in stature, and in spirit. The word of God is with all who would listen; indeed, it is there even for the ones who do not heed. For in this life, or the next, the spirit must try to perfect the deeds and thoughts as to the final return. To some, the trips to human form are many. To others it is but a stop so briefly along the way. The love of God is a guide to take you across the swollen stream, and the rocky pathways, on to a glorious ending that words will never describe.

Love thy God.

September 28, 1980

Question: I would like to know if I should be questioning my Guides, or am I to accept that which has been given to me by them?

QUAKER: By all means, you may question us anytime you wish. The truth you seek is available to us, and you shall receive it as the truth. All things will not be agreeable to everyone, as it is hard to change someone's mind when they believe something to be true when you are telling them otherwise. You must keep your search for knowledge on the highest levels. Frivolous things will not be acceptable, as our concern for you is to bring you wisdom. Only as you widen your knowledge of the world you live in, must you also widen your knowledge of the worlds beyond.

Question: I sense the presence of yet another Guide with me today. Am I right? (The writing was unusually small, and I felt differently at times while writing).

QUAKER: Yes my friend, you can tell when you are with another. It will be my job to help you see through some of these problems. My name is Quaker and you will hear from me again. It is not necessary for you to call upon me, as there are many sitting in on your daily writing sessions. Keep up your writing, as you shall uncover many things and great wisdom can be yours. But you must take it slowly to absorb the meaning. As the light brightens, so shall the darkened corners be clear to you.

September 29, 1980

Question: Can you tell me is world conflict near because of the war that is going on in the Middle East?

MARTHA: The facts of the Middle East wars are that they will not bring themselves to live with one another as neighbours. They have lost the sight of God's word, as they hold the ownership of land and wealth above God. The other nations of the world will not want to be drawn into a full-scale world war over these few small countries that cannot live in peace with one another. It is possible that the war will spread to other Middle Eastern countries, but it would be foolish for the Western world to get involved with this now.

Question: If worldwide conflict was to happen what would be expected of us?

The possibilities are so many that we cannot possibly cover them all. However, if worldwide war was to prevail it would most certainly affect everyone, as the spoils of war are for the conqueror. This would drive the leaders of many nations to win at all cost. Many young men and women would be called upon to place their lives in jeopardy, as they would have to take up arms to protect their homelands. All is lost in a war like this, as everyone will inflict casualties on the other. Many God fearing souls will lose their lives or their homes to a war that should never exist. The act of war upon one another is a great sin unto God, as he made man in His image. But man has become unrecognizable to God; for it is love and not war that man lives his life for on this planet. Many things happen to change the shape of history, and few are constructive. It is unfortunate that man must have these conflicts with his fellow man, to settle that which should be settled in prayer. The Lord God on high is not able to stop this conflict without that He takes sides with one of his children. For all God's creatures are his children. It is for mankind to learn to live in peace and harmony, if the universal love of God is to be in the heart of all mankind. God so loved us all that he sent His only son to save the world from sin. But today, the thought of God or His son is far from the minds of many who would set the world on fire once more. Many a man would want life to go on as before, for it is not all men who wish to wage war upon their fellow man. Conflicts have been present on earth since time began, but they were minor in nature and they were between man and beast. Slowly they became a part of living between mankind. Only when we put all thoughts of war aside, will world peace return. For he who smites his brother, strikes a blow against his Father. War will come unto you, and may God have mercy on those that lie in its path.

Question: Will this war be worldwide in a short time?

The elements are there, the urgency to settle this is upon you now.

September 30, 1980

Question: Can you tell me what changes will take place in the writings? Will we be getting into deeper meanings of life?

MARTHA: You are anxious to learn, but all in good time. As you progress, you will be given many of the secrets of life. The only thing you must do now is to continue with your studies so as to prepare for the ultimate when it is available to you. You see, as the tree grows so do its branches reach out. So as man's knowledge grows, it too will reach for more, and its roots will require more food to let it bloom into maturity. Be not in a hurry, as there is plenty of time for you. Only as the information can be used, can it be given. Your book will have to be started soon, as you have many lectures that you can use. As you progress you will be given more. Be careful of those who you divulge your information to, as some may not be able to accept it as you do. The glory of God is still the uppermost principle that you must content yourself with, as it is through the glory of God that this is all possible. Go unto the land and seek the knowledge you wish, and then seek your answers here, for it will be given unto you. Be of good heart as the only thing that can stop this knowledge is you. You have demonstrated the sincere want of knowledge as you have been writing for almost a year now. Do not ever let this gift lie dormant, as it is a gift from God. The only ones who can receive as you do, grow in God's mercy and shall be held in a kindly light. For darkness will never stop thee again. Only as the light of day leaves all others, you may see that the way is clear. Stray not from thy Father's house, as you have had the door opened unto you. Carry the word of God to all that would listen, as you carry the salvation of your world. The return to the laws of man will bring a return to the laws of God. But, if it is not forthcoming, the laws of God must once again be felt by mankind, as it must be done. Give unto others that which has been given to you, for it is for all mankind to know. Love thy God and thy life will be full of joy and happiness. Give not unto others that which has not been given unto you, for false prophets will cleanse thee not. The way is clear, go now and do thy bidding.

October 3, 1980

Question: The other night, I awoke with the sound of someone calling to me. It was the voice of a woman, and when I asked who was there and what did they want, the voice stopped. Is it possible that someone was talking to me or was it just a dream?

MARTHA: No Peter, you were not dreaming. Sarah wanted to come to you with a message. She would have left this as a thought in your subconscious, only you must have awakened and sensed her presence. You may well start to receive some of your messages this way very soon, as you seem ready for this change. Do not be alarmed when it happens, as it will be your Guides that will come to you. Your prayers for protection will keep discarnates away. So do not be alarmed, as no harm shall come to you. The experience of talking to one on this plane is gifted to very few. You will enjoy these encounters as time goes by. Many things are yet to be said, but all in good time. We will keep you busy, as there are many things to do. Start to write your book, it must be done.

. October 4, 1980

MARTHA: God so loved us all He gave His only begotten son for us. Do you still love thy God? Many souls cannot answer a question such as this, for as to the loss of a loved one there seems no cause great enough. You have lost a son, and you have asked why. It is now that you will begin to understand. The return of the spirit is likened to the return home after a long stay away, and for that spirit the draw is very strong. In the newborn it is still there as the spirit has not yet settled into the life that he supports. When things are wrong, it is often the case where the spirit will leave the new body and return to the sanctity of the spirit plane from whence he came. But all thought has been given to remaining, the difficulties that will prevail, and the sorrow felt by the family as the infant tries to grow with the defect that he is aware of. At this point, if karma is due, and a longer life of suffering is needed to repay, life goes on. But if the decision to return is made, that this life will only further burden the family, then the spirit shall return. The decision is made with the help of guides that know the circumstances awaiting this child. To place a burden upon a family that has children to care for and no other need is called for karma, all will be better if the spirit returns. The loss of the infant is a great loss, but the loss of that child at full growth is yet a greater loss. God does not punish the parents of the newborn child by having the spirit return. It is a blessing on the infant not to go through life as an inflicted soul. God's love has many faces; some show sorrow, some show happiness, but in the end they shall be with God.

October 7, 1980

INFINITY: You shall give of this earth that which you have taken. All mankind will have a mission to perform before they accept a chance to return once more to the spirit plane. You have your mission. You must complete it if your spirit is to return. Martha is not with us today, although we do have a message. You are to take your writings and begin your work. You have much to work with. The time draws near when all should be finished on this book. You should worry not how it will be published, as it will be given that you will meet with someone who has the knowledge of this. Our communication is poor today. You may need to rest.

Go with God.

*It never seemed to fail, that if I was tired or not able to settle into a session, some comment was made to this effect.

October 8, 1980

MARTHA: You are to go about your work, as all things shall come to pass when you are ready. The work of God is something that must be done. As you begin your writings now, you will be receiving a little more in the way of lectures that you will want for this book. The first one is in your mind now and you must go on with it first. There will be more, possibly many more. You will have to read them over and pick out the lectures that will hold a message for all. Then, you must also write a lead to the book, an introduction.

We may be able to help you there also, but you must be able to come up with many things that have happened that will give you this introduction. When all is finished, a publisher will be sought out and your book of lectures will be a thing of reality. But the work does not stop there, as there will be more books and more lectures. Then, a number of lectures, as you will be called upon to make. You will always have someone at your side when this happens, to help you with the lesson you will preach. Keep your daily writings up, at all costs, as you must never let this channel close. Your gift is a gift to mankind. You must use it as such. Many months have gone by since we started on this and Sara will be happy to hear when you have started your book. There are many things to unfold for you my friend. The act of God is but a start of the things you shall learn. You have much to work with now and much more to come, so on with it my friend. You have a busy time ahead. May God's love be with you always as your guiding light, for as the darkness draws near, the shaft of divine light shall lead thy way, and thy staff shall hold thee against thyself. Dedicate thy life and works to thy God, as you must finish that which lies before you, before you are able to journey much farther. When you need assistance, pray to God and your prayers will be answered, for there are many who watch over you. Go with God my friend.

Question: The phrase "the act of God" is used many times. Can you define this for me?

It is the feeling of contentment to the Lord above.

October 10, 1980

MARTHA: Peter, you are not going to get as much done as you want this winter, as there are a few more things you are going to be asked to do. Be careful that you do not get too involved, as your health has to be taken into consideration. Many people may seek you out for readings and it may also come that you will be invited to lecture in another town. Your book has to be foremost in your projects, as it is your wish and ours that you proceed on with it. Deliver yourself not unto thy brother, for him to take advantage, but go there and seek your goal. There are many things that are asked of you. God's work must always be looked upon as a duty. You have come a long way in your year of involvement, and it still has a long way to go yet. Many more doors will be opened, but first you must catch up to yourself. The word of God reaches many people. The way in which it is delivered varies with the wind. Yours is but one of the ways to spread the word. Give not that which ye cannot give, but give back which ye can ask God's help for, for He alone shall grant thy wishes. Twilight is the time of contentment, but God's light is always.

October 11, 1980

MARTHA: Only as we walk with God do we walk in his footsteps. Time eternal shall be forever and we must fulfill our lives to live in God's grace throughout eternity. The glory of God cannot only be seen, but it can be heard from a voice within. Listen, and when it is heard, heed thy voice and live as God would have you live, in peace and harmony with all mankind. The love of God should make a tremendous difference in your daily life, as He will help you through the difficulties you come upon. Faith in God will remove many barriers in life, as many have witnessed. Only as we come nearer to God do we find that contentment that man needs to live his life in total harmony. Man's love for his fellow man is but an extension of the love that is God. As we journey life's road, we come on to many events that will try this love, but the true love shall remain and weather the events. A gift of life brings with it a gift of love, for is it not so that even the unwanted child is loved by someone? God's love is the strongest element man shall ever stand before. It shall be all consuming as in the end it shall be as one. The glory of God be with you, my friend.

On the morning of October 5, 1980 I had received the strangest writing yet. It was as though I was drawing many odd shaped symbols. I cannot re-create them now; however, when I asked who had sent this message, I was told it was the ancient wise one of Egypt. I was told that the message will be revealed in the future as it is for the future.

Question: Can you tell me more of the origin of the strange writings I received this past week?

SPIRIT: Yes, you were in contact with a learned one of old Egypt. You must remember that they were the first civilized people on earth that communicated with the written word. You are right when you thought they might have been from Atlantis, as they fled the holocaust and journeyed to Egypt and many other eastern countries. Their writing is unlike anything you will find. The answers are locked in the memory of time. Man will only unlock this when he finds

God. Only as man becomes more Godlike, shall the answers to many things be revealed to him. The answers to many things lie in the depth of the oceans of time. Many things will happen that will bring about change on earth. One of these changes will uncover a great amount of hidden knowledge, as it is buried under the sands of time. Many of the secrets are written on tablets hidden on the site of the great pyramid. Only as man is drawn closer to God will the pathway to this hidden knowledge be found. Many of man's problems could be solved by the secrets, and many of the troubled ways of life should be removed from your world. The test of time will bring joy to all who wait, only for the final ending. Go about your ways, but beware the changes to come, for he who shall smite thy brother, shall he be smitten. He who shows a love of God shall be taken into his kingdom. The Lord God is holy. He awaits the return of his flock. For he who journeys forth shall in time return unto Me, so sayeth our Lord.

This was signed in a signature I could not make out.

October 13, 1980

SPIRIT: As you go about your work, think of His work, so it shall be your work. The spirit flame is never out, for it burns always. Give of your whole being, for is it not the wishes of thy Father? Place unto the altar of God thy life, and do the bidding of thy God for it is meant to be. Try to think of the suffering of the souls of mankind and of the peace that can be brought unto them. Never will the pathway darken if the word of God remains in your heart, for eternity shall be yours. Only the test of time shall bring the mortal body to rest, but the spirit shall live in spirit form until the moment it becomes as one with creation. You have been given a gift of teaching. You must use the gift as it was given to us all here, and we are but passing it on to you, so that you will pass it on to the living souls about you. Your progression into the yet unknown shall be that of the blind being able to see the light of day, for so it will seem to you. For what you shall see you shall be blessed with that knowledge to understand, and it shall be as one. Go and seek thy place as it is being prepared for thee. Give unto him who needs the light to guide him, the words of encouragement so as to stay thy path. Love thy God as He loves thee and the pathway shall be made light for all who follow you.

October 15, 1980

MARTHA: Yes Peter, there is a message today. As you go about your chosen work you will feel the need for something else in your daily routine. The work of God is in you. You must find your place. Give not that which you cannot, but use that which is given to you, as this is going to be a great sermon. The cross bears the scars of Jesus, and all mankind also bear those scars, for the sin of man is likened to the scars of the cross, and mankind has to cleanse the soul for repentance. Man is an earthly creature now, as he has removed himself from that of God. But his return is a must, and he can return only in the purest state. The salvation of mankind will come from his return to God and godly things, for he was a creation of God before he became a creature of the earth. The will of God is that all mankind should live in a world of peace and brotherhood, but the warring that continues takes man further from his God. Many lifetimes will be lost in karma for he who slays his brother. Know in your heart that God commands peace.

October 20, 1980

MARTHA: Only he who spreads the word of God shall be looked on with reverence. Many people spread the word but care not from where the word came. Go about your life as a messenger, but carry only that which is worthy of thy task. Only as the word is given, shall it be put into practice, for it is not a holy vow unless it has been uttered by God. Beware the prophets that bring you words you cannot accept. Surely God in his glory shall see to his children. Your concern over that which you have heard is in no way necessary, for that which you have heard is not to be. Follow the words you have received and spread them about for they are from a good source. Try not to judge those that bring forth words of another kind for they know not from where they come. Pray for thy protection and it shall be given, but pray not, and the mind is open to the devil's disciples, for they too wish to spread their fear to anyone who will listen. The word of God is the highest you can receive and lo, you have received it many times. Your foundation is strong. Your strength is that of a mountain, for neither wind nor storm shall move it from its path. Be as you are, for all shall be opened unto you, and you shall spread the word of God. Worry not for that which is claimed to be, but only for that, that shall be. Live and love thy God and thy place awaits thee.

As Told To Me

October 21, 1980

MARTHA: There are those who would have you believe that this is not possible. However, we know it is true. Do not let anyone discourage you from continuing with your writing for much would be lost. That which you receive is for all mankind, but all will never listen. It is only the few that hold the faith in a greater hereafter that can accept this form of communication. Do not settle for what you have received till now, but continue forever to receive in some way the messages of God, so they may be shared with mankind. Your concern for others is very noble, but they must have the faith to believe in their own ability to separate that which is chaff from that which is wheat. You must continue to speak out, as you have, against that which is evil sent. For, it is no harder to be in contact with the spiritual good than it is to be contacted by the spiritual damned. The way is clear for you. You are only to follow thy guides, for your direction is that of the prophet, and you shall speak the true meaning of God's words. Worry not that many will seem to follow that which you deem as false, but will follow that which they believe to be true. The true teachers shall know thy work is true, and shall go forth and spread the word. Carry on, my friend, for the journey shall never be without a companion, as we journey with you.

October 22, 1980

SPIRIT: Only as we give of ourselves do we receive. The smallest things can often bring the biggest joy. As one reflects, so he reflects his feelings for others. Many things that seem undistinguishable to us are clouded merely by our own mind, as we do not see them as we should. So it is with many things that are spoken; they too can be misconstrued as to the meaning. The human mind should be controlled by the spirit, but if the spirit is not given a chance to be accepted, the body must function by the brain alone, without the guidance of spiritual assistance. Often the spirit is trapped in a body that does not wish to function in a manner that the spirit desires. At this time, a conflict will often occur that brings about a sudden change in the person, as the spirit gains control. Few of the spiritual souls ever get to express themselves as fully as they wish, as they are governed by the events about them. As you go about many tasks that seem too great, a sudden surge of energy is often felt. This is the spirit in its attempt to help and give that needed assistance you require. The spirit is a very complex thing, as it wishes to express itself through the person who shares it with God.

October 23, 1980

MARTHA: You are not to worry over other people's actions. Trust in your Guides and in the word of God and all things shall be made clear to you. Give of yourself when you feel the need, for it is never right to always wait to be asked. Man's inhumanity to his fellow man will be with us for many generations to come. Only through the increased number of souls that are contacted and carry that message on, will a widening of the circle of believers in God's law happen. Your contribution to this can be great if you do as your heart desires. You have the opportunity to contact many with your writings. The unbeliever is God's child even though he is lost in his search for survival, for it is through God that he shall find mercy. As the circle widens so shall the universal love of God take control of the world's problems that cause strife and warfare among people today. God wants his children to live in peace, but if peace cannot be attained, the Spirit may live in mortal fear in each ensuing lifetime as the Spirit reaches for the perfect union with God. Mankind must learn to live with man before he can ever reach for the union with his Creator, for man is his image, not his double. World peace will someday be a reality, for it is a must if we are to return to God as one. It is through achieving this peace that we shall progress our spirit to its final ending.

October 24, 1980

MARTHA: Will you please walk with God, for it is in His shadow true peace will be found? You are not to go forth without the true feeling of God's love, for it is the strength of this love that will guide you throughout your life. We are here to offer you our help, but it is God who commands your love, for He so loves his children. Go into the city of darkness and ye shall bring a light, and when the light appears, all men will wonder at its being. The true test shall come with confrontation, and the strength of your soul shall be that of David, for every obstacle can be that of a giant. Go not to do your bidding, but go to do God's bidding and you shall find the sheep, and you shall spare the lamb. Our Father is not in Heaven only, for He is everywhere that the eye can see, the ear can hear and the body can touch. God is eternal. He is a living being through his conception of all living things. Many of man's objects of living proof are but a mirror of God's love of man, for he is in His image. Only as we draw our lives close to the ways of our Lord God do we find peace of mind and peace in our heart to accept that man is not His equal. But by following His words we may return unto Him as one. Give of the heart for it is fulfilling to the soul. Mankind will someday return to harmony with his fellow man and will bathe in God's love.

October 27, 1980

MARTHA: Your father is always listening; you must trust in His words. Fear not the multitudes that draw away from Christ, but take comfort in the many who see the need for God in their lives. Man shall someday destroy himself in his quest for power, as he holds himself up as a God to others. No one but the followers of God's law shall be spared the fury that shall descend upon mankind. For it is now upon us, the time of man's conquest of mankind, and he will not wait until he is in full knowledge of that which he does. Many lives are lost to the sounds of power rumbling in a land they own not. Man was never meant to go unto his neighbour and take that which he desired. Many lessons have been learned by past civilizations that you cannot control that which you do not own. Man has warred against his fellow man for many centuries, but the awesome weight of his sword has never been as heavy as now. Man's ability to destroy that which was built to last has surmounted that of the giant and the sling, for lo the force is awesome. Will man never learn that his mission on earth is to learn and do bidding unto his Lord and Master? The endless wars on earth have set brother unto brother but they do not recognize each other. Given the opportunity, man must learn to love thy neighbour, before it is too late to save the world from itself.

October 28, 1980

Question: The interest shown by many in the second coming of Christ is very strong now. Is this to happen in my lifetime?

MARTHA: You may feel that Christ comes at any time, for his coming, and going, are set by no one. As for his return in the flesh, that is another matter. Yes, many expect to see the Heavens divide and our Lord Jesus descend from the Heavens to save them from the ways of the earthly sins. Man has many things to learn, many things to overcome, before he will witness our Lord Jesus. It is spoken in the Bible, that He shall rise and take you unto His home. But it does not say He will make a spectacle of this. Truly, Jesus does touch the hearts of many every day, and for those, it is truly the second coming for them. When one finds the true love of God in his heart, then he too has experienced the second coming. Do not get the second coming confused with the return of the spirit, or with the Heavens opening and a host of angels coming down to live on this earth again, for there is a better place, and we dwell there now with our Lord, and so shall all who call Him holy. For Heaven is a place to come into oneness with the creation, and then to oneness with the Creator. Man will have to get along as best he can without God's presence in person, as you would say. The presence of God is with many souls, though, at all times. You can feel the presence of God, or of the holy Son of God, Jesus, at any moment of your life. As you are drawn closer to your quest for peace at heart, you will find Him always waiting for you to call upon Him. Give not into the ways of mankind who want to see only the physical being of God before they will accept that there truly is a God. But, go about your way and do as the Lord wishes of you and give not into the weakness of man but hold strong to the workings of the Lord's deeds in mankind. If God so wished to open the Heavens and descend onto earth, He would do so at any time, not when man expects to see Him. The Bible holds many secrets that man has never translated from the many words of God. Many will remain as secret today as when they were uttered, for all things are not spoken to every man but for some they hold great meaning. Trust not that which is not felt in the heart, for it is here that God shall make his second coming. All mankind shall feel the coming at one point in their lives. Others will feel the presence often. Trust your life unto God, for He alone shall welcome you.

October 30, 1980

MARTHA: Think not that you stand alone, for God stands with you. Try to remember that one who carries God's love in his heart, is never alone. In the darkest corners of the earth God shall stand beside you. Go and tarry not over the frivolous things, but live your life as it was meant to be. As the wind blows in the storm so shall it clear away the clouds that obscure that which you cannot see. Many things are done to attract man's interest in the holy way, but few really know the meaning of the sign. It is known only in the heart of the beholder. This knowledge is in all mankind but few ever use the power they possess. You must be aware of the existence of God, and of evil forces, for it is not uncommon to have the evil forces take possession of the soul. Your prayers for protection are always heard, and you will always be protected from this evil force. Many new things are yet to be revealed to you, but not yet, as you have much to do and much to catch up on. Your thoughts are often on your book. This is good as it will soon start and as it draws near completion, you will find yet another inner peace that you never knew existed. Deep in the inner soul there lies the truth of man's existence, and many answers could be obtained if man could reach the inner soul. Your mission in this life was to bring understanding to mankind, and this shall come about. Your way is clearing. Your goal is God.

November 1, 1980

MARTHA: Will the love of God be all it takes to save mankind? No, it must also be balanced with the love of your fellow man. For he who smites his fellow man, he too smites his God. Man must learn to live in closer harmony with his fellow man and with the creation around him if he is ever to gain the holy breath. Mankind must cease his conflict with man and beast, for it is against God's law. The beasts no longer prey on mankind, such as when he was hunted by the huge beasts of past civilizations; however, man still slays the beast for the sport of the kill. The balance of nature between man and beast must once again be felt, for it was not God's wish to have the beast hunted and slain. So too does man slay his brother. World conflict is always about, as man has never learned to live in peace. There are many lands where war is unheard of, but they too slay the beast. Many things will have to happen to bring the balance of nature back to its proper place. Man cannot be all consuming of the universe without paying a terrible price.

You must be careful of the words you speak, for many will understand not the words you utter. Give not only to those that are wanting, but give to him that asks not.

November 3, 1980

MARTHA: You are not too far from your goal. Things are going to make way for that which you feel necessary. The Lord's work shall be done. Go unto the fields of life for there lay the answers to so many of life's questions. He who lives by the word of God need fear not those who would do him harm, for he will always be in the house of God. Only if you fear life, will you not succeed in building a strong base to live on. For fear is but to have little faith, and to have little faith is to question God. Man has many faces and few are the trusting face of faith. As you go into life's mainstream you will find it hard to justify that which others hold to be true, but what is truth, unless it was uttered first by God? The words of many that follow the work of God are confused, and utter false meaning to His words, for they know not what they speak. Many a sermon is preached unto deaf ears, for its meaning has been changed to suit the sermon. Change not that which you receive, for thou art being given the true meaning of God's commandments. Walk freely unto the fields and harvest the crop of life, for the time for picking is here. Those whose lives are at blossom will follow thee to the kingdom of Heaven. Give to God that which you will give to man, and He shall receive you as a man of God.

November 4, 1980

MARTHA: Keep in company with God, for it is there you shall find your answers. The best you can do is not always the best you can expect from yourself. For it is not *what* is accomplished, but *how* it is accomplished that counts. To take another at a disadvantage is not the way to achieve that which you feel is important. To help someone else along the way to your own goal is but to extend the hand of God to others that need it. For it is through the living that God shall send His help to the ones who need Him, and to those that pray for it. Many a master has been made from a kindly deed expressed by God through a fellow man. The act of kindness is not something that should be taken lightly, for it was sent to answer a need. When you help your brother along the way, you help yourself one more step. The love of God that should reside in all mankind is not kindled often enough to set the flames to that of light, for if you could but see beyond the next darkened bend, you would feel the need to love God and your brother more surely than ever before. Man has built a fence around God's house, but he forgot to leave the gate to enter. To some the gate does not exist, but to others the fence does not exist. Do not fence your life off from that which you must someday find the opening for. Forgiveness is mine, sayeth the Lord, and I shall forgive those who come unto me with love in their hearts and goodness in their deeds unto others. The road to Heaven is paved in gold or strewn with embers. You shall make the journey as hard or as glorious as you wish, but to find that which man strives for, you must, one way or another, travel this road. If you have strewn your pathway with the embers of your misdeeds, then you must correct them before you journey any further. But, if you have found the road opens unto you in a blaze of glorious colour and the pathway is clear for you, your journey nears its final ending, for you have found a way to paradise and to your Heavenly host. God awaits those who come unto him with love in their heart, for he alone can bid them welcome. The final chapter has been written only when you have found atonement, for it is here you shall become one with God and live as we once had existed, as one with God. Keep thy peace with man and thy love with God, and when the journey starts, the way will be clear. The journey shall be like none other you shall ever remember, for the beauty is beyond the beholder to explain. For God has created this as a place to dwell and to receive His children unto Him.

November 5, 1980

MARTHA: You must go about your work very soon. This book must be written. Only time will tell if there are to be any more, but the first must be. Only as we draw nearer to God do we fear not, that which to some means so much. As we grow older we know that our life grows shorter, and our time to make our mark on the world around us grows smaller. Your books shall be your mark, for they alone shall leave your name and work in print for many to read. Only you can tell if you have left a lasting mark on your fellow man, as others will attest after you have returned. Man has a duty to help his fellow man, but above all, he has a duty to God. By helping his fellow man he is doing his duty to God. Life is a precious thing and it must be cherished while there is still time to enjoy it. But it is of God, and as all things of God, must one day return unto Him. You have much to do as you have many things to put in place and your book will take more time than you realize. Walk with God in your heart my friend, for He alone holds our lives in His hand.

November 7, 1980

MARTHA: You have taken the first step, now go on with your book. You must spend the time you can in writing and preparing the many lectures that you will include in it. There is much happiness here, that you have finally started this book. There will be many times that you will need help. If you do, just listen, for we will be there at all times. This book will be sought by many, as it will relate your experiences with the subject that is now becoming increasingly more popular. Your world must learn to accept spiritualism as its rightful identity, for it is now that people should be turning to God for help, before it is too late. For many, your work will seem as a fictitious story, and they will ridicule your sincerity; however, there are those who will know it is true and will share your experience in their own way. To light the path is but to be the guide for many to pass this way. For without the light, the darkness is never left. Man has lived in darkness for many ages, but he must look up and accept that the life hereafter is here now. To those who choose to follow, the way is open, "for you must approach the door and knock, and it shall be opened unto you."

November 8, 1980

INFINITY: Your thoughts are true, your reasoning is right; many of life's problems are put before us by ourselves. The messages you have been receiving are of a source that cannot be questioned as being misleading. Only through your own mind could you attempt to put change to these words, and you know this does not work. Be not concerned over that which someone else is writing, for many messages are sent to many people at many times. To some they cannot separate that which should be cast aside, for they know not the truth in their hearts. Your receiving of these messages comes through from both good and evil spirits. How one accepts them on your side is something that only you have control over. From your many lifetimes past, you have been receiving transitional messages, many, many times. Your own mind, and your guardian mind, the subconscious, will tell you when you have been contacted by those who make a game of placing fear into the hearts of man. Be not afraid of truth, but be wary of false truth and slander for it is around you always. Let your mind free, and the entities of many will follow you to possess that which they feel they can control. God gave man a mind of his own to use, to judge that which he deems necessary.

*This message was signed with the symbol for Infinity.

November 10, 1980

INFINITY: You must keep on the alert for those who bring you false prophecy. Your conscience will be your guide. Follow it well. The work of God is said to be masked in many ways, but it will hold a true feeling in the heart, if it is so. Prophets bring words that are said to be of God, but are false and should be turned loose to the wind. Never accept that which the heart does not accept, for it is the testing point of our emotions. Many a false tale can be made to sound as truth but if tried in the heart, the true meaning will prevail. In the end there shall be false prophets who will bring their words to the flock. Beware, for it is those who follow that life that shall bear hardship. God is all-powerful and is forgiving, but you must be aware that to some His words fall on deaf ears, for they knoweth not what they say. Be at one with God, and your heart shall be your guide, for I am truth, sayeth the Lord. *Signed Infinity symbol*

Question: Might I ask the identity of the wise one, who signs his messages in this manner?

INFINITY: You must know by now that the identity means little to the message, for it is the message that holds the answer, not the identity of the sender.

In Conclusion

I want to express my own feelings about this book and its possible acceptance. I feel that it will fall into three categories: first there will be those who will disbelieve all possibility of this ever happening. They are content in having their lives spelled out for them by tradition, never attempting something new or letting the mere thought of something as far out as this hold even a moment's concentration. To these people, I do not wish in any way to have them feel that I am trying to impose my thoughts on them, for who am I to judge?

To many others, it will be another in the many confirmations they have had in their belief in the spiritual realm. To these people, reincarnation and the next plane are very commonplace in their everyday lives. To the spiritually inclined, all information on this subject is eagerly sought. These people have found a certain contentment in their lives, that only they can share.

Lastly, but far from the least, is the final group; for these are the ones who stand at the brink. They are the ones who wish to know about their past. They are also greatly concerned with their future and they await the light to illuminate their way. Their belief in a superior being is strong, but they cannot accept what the many religious teachings of today have to offer.

The proliferation of religions that exist today must add greatly to the indifference that we are witnessing in our reaction to our fellow man. When we have large groups of fanatical followers that want to dominate the world at all cost, surely we must be on a collision course of mammoth proportion. God must have meant for mankind to exist in harmony, not in fear of what his neighbour might be doing. If, and it's a big "IF", mankind could come together and respect one another's religious beliefs and live in peace, what a truly wonderful world this could be. What is now being spent on building an army and protecting one's borders could be spent on improving life for all those who need help just to survive from day to day. Collectively, we could improve the state of MOTHER EARTH by correcting the harm we have done over the last few centuries. Imagine what clean water would mean to those who search just to quench their thirst with a few drops of water. Then there are those who know the air they breathe is unfit for human life, thanks to the chemicals that have destroyed its purity. So much could be done for the betterment of mankind, but when will it happen? Will this be the generation that will begin the correction or will it be just one more that takes us deeper into despair? Time could possibly be running out for mankind. We were meant to populate this earth as God had created it not to destroy it.

Another thing that comes to mind is the reference to *"man's inhumanity to his fellow man"*. Surely this points to the unending wars and oppressions we humans endure and perpetuate on this earth. If it is not a small nation threatening its neighbour, it is the *"Superpowers"* rattling their sabres. In the message of September 29, 1980, it refers to the *"setting fire of the world once more"*. It does not take a great deal of imagination to draw a parallel between this wording and the possibility of nuclear war. If you read this carefully, it says "*once more*", but when did this happen before? Would those who believe that history repeats itself be prepared to accept this? Maybe God did in fact give us a mind to think beyond our limited view of life in this world. Hell was used in a reference to life, and what more hellish thing to imagine than for the whole world to erupt into a nuclear holocaust. Man somehow has to overcome his inability to live at peace with his brother, for we are all a part of God's family.

Perhaps in some small way this book will help in bringing about enough interest to attract others to this subject. There are many prominent authors writing on the spiritual significance of current world conditions, and I do not include myself among these talented people. "*Blinders were made for beasts of burden, not for man, but for some, they will always have to be led*". Man stands tall when he has to stand alone and be counted. Some, unfortunately, cannot find a place to stand. For me, this book has been a learning experience, and I look forward to what the future may hold.

So now my friends, "***go quietly, and listen to the whisper of the wind, and when you know what it says, you are indeed attuned to creation***".

About The Author

Peter Watson's entry into writing a book does not replicate anything else he has ever accomplished. With only entrance grade education and hard work, he has overcome any shortfalls he may have had with his schooling. Peter's working life started quite young—first as a paperboy, then as a delivery boy for a corner store. At 14, Peter went to work for a car dealership, and from there to an apprenticeship as a Motor Machinist at an automotive machine shop. After many years working in the shop, Peter moved on to another town as a branch manager for the company. Several years later he became an agent with a Life Insurance Company.

Like many others, the "Midlife Crisis" took its toll on Peter and at 50, his first marriage ended, and he started out on a new journey.

Peter met his current wife, Joy and together they spent a few years RV'ing between Florida in the winter and a return to Ontario for the summer. Peter's sudden turn of health brought them back to Ontario to settle in Guelph where Joy resumed her massage therapy profession, and Peter designed and built specialty tables for massage therapists.

After Peter retired from business, he found himself with time on his hands and decided it was now time to retrieve the manuscript, *As Told To Me* that he had channeled so long ago, and bring it to fruition.

Peter W Watson

www.ingramcontent.com/pod-product-compliance
Lightning Source LLC
Chambersburg PA
CBHW071715090426
42738CB00009B/1780